Stephanie and
Charlie Wetzel

HarperCollins
LEADERSHIP
AN IMPRINT OF HarperCollins

# THE
# SPANX
# STORY

T0001457

## What's Underneath the Incredible Success
## of Sara Blakely's Billion-Dollar Empire

Published by HarperCollins Leadership, an imprint of HarperCollins Focus LLC.

Published in association with Yates & Yates: https://www.yates2.com/.

Book design by Aubrey Khan, Neuwirth & Associates.

ISBN 978-1-4002-1617-8 (eBook)
ISBN 978-1-4002-1611-6 (HC)

Library of Congress Control Number: 2020941781

20 21 22 23 LSC 10 9 8 7 6 5 4 3 2 1

# CONTENTS

**1998**

Sara Blakely cuts off the feet of her control top pantyhose, sparking an idea that changes the way women wear clothes.

**2000**

Sara obtains a patent and perfects a prototype for Spanx.

**2000**

Spanx are included on the "Oprah's Favorite Things" list.

**2002**

Sara brings on CEO Laurie Ann Goldman.

**2002**

Spanx sales through QVC reach $8 million, representing approximately 30 percent of their revenue.

**2003**

Spanx crosses the pond to launch in the UK.

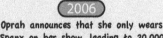
**2006**

Oprah announces that she only wears Spanx on her show, leading to 20,000 orders in one day.

## 2020
James Corden announces that his new year's resolution is to do one show without wearing Spanx.

## 2017
Spanx introduces Arm Tights.

## 2016
Sara Blakely returns as Spanx CEO.

## 2013
Sara promises to give more than half of her wealth to charitable causes.

## 2012
Sara appears on the cover of Forbes as the youngest self-made female billionaire.

## 2010
Spanx launches its men's line.

## 2008
Spanx expands its offerings with the launch of the Bra-llelujah, an instant hit in the lingerie marketplace.

"Anyone can become an inventor as long as they keep an open and inquiring mind and never overlook the possible significance of an accident or apparent failure."

—PATSY O'CONNELL SHERMAN,
Scientist and Inventor of Scotchgard

# CHAPTER ONE

# A BILLION-DOLLAR IDEA

**S**ara Blakely never set out to revolutionize and revive a dy-
ing industry, create a new category of clothing, or become
a billionaire at age forty-one. As she has told it, all she wanted
was to make a good impression at a party.

Standing by her closet door, Sara looked down at the invitation in her hand. For the young, single twenty-seven-year-old,
still new to the big city, an invitation to a big social event in a
swanky rooftop bar would have been a huge deal. Like many
other recent transplants to Atlanta, Georgia, in 1998, Sara had
moved there for work. A few months after relocating, she would
have met and interacted with many of her coworkers in the
offices of Danka, a national business machinery company.

Sara spent several days each week outside of Atlanta, visiting
small cities and towns like the one where she'd grown up and
been offered her first real job out of college. There at the
Danka headquarters, in her cozy beach hometown of Clearwater, Florida, she had started selling fax machines door-to-door.

But it didn't take long for her work ethic and sales results to attract the attention of management. A fast learner and skilled salesperson, she was soon called upon to guide and help others in her department. And when it became clear that Sara was also a skilled instructor, Danka offered her a promotion—out of sales and into the training department at the regional office in Georgia. Now she spent her time teaching other salespeople throughout the country how to get a foot in the door, connect with potential customers, and close the deal.

Naturally outgoing and charismatic, Sara normally had no problem making friends. The invitation to this social gathering created a high-stakes opportunity for Sara. And it had to be more energizing than drinking office coffee while discussing sales strategies for office equipment.

Like everyone preparing to meet new people, Sara knew first impressions matter a great deal. Of course, when she walked into the room, it was important to look her best: professional, put-together, appropriate. The clothes she chose needed to meet those criteria. But it was even more crucial to look *confident* and *relaxed.* To appear confident and relaxed, she needed an outfit that would enable her to *feel* confident and relaxed. And, honestly, was that too much to ask?

## That Moment in Front of the Closet

Sara has described in dozens of interviews that moment in front of her closet. And, according to her, the answer to that question was a resounding yes—it *was* too much to ask. Over and over, her eyes kept being drawn to a pair of brand-new white pants that would match perfectly with the light summer blouse and strappy sandals that she had in mind for the party.

But the pants, which had looked amazing on the hanger and beautiful in the dressing room mirror, had yet to be worn out of the house. In fact, they'd hung there in the closet for *eight months* with the tags still on. For one thing, she said that seeing the trousers was a reminder that she'd paid too much for them—nearly $100—not to wear them. According to Sara, her attention immediately went to every imperfection, making her feel insecure and unsure of herself. So, every time, she ended up taking them off, hanging them back up, and changing into something else before leaving the house.

Picturing Sara in 1998, at just twenty-seven, she was pretty, slender, and petite. Her long blonde hair, white teeth, and casual vibe made her look like she'd grown up on the beach—which in fact she had. In her hometown of Clearwater Beach, Florida, Sara said she grew up where everyone wore shorts, flip-flops, and swimsuits—for eleven months out of the year. The professional attire that businesswomen wore in Atlanta was much more structured, formal, and *expensive.* "High fashion and design were foreign to me," Sara said of her life before Atlanta.

Everything moved faster in Atlanta, too (aside from the traffic). People walked fast. Serious people in serious clothing strode purposefully to do serious work for serious employers. The men tended to wear dark-colored suits, ties, and shiny dress shoes. Even on Casual Fridays, they all wore a uniform of sorts, of khaki trousers and golf shirts. But the women's attire really stood out. Many of them seemed to put a lot of effort into looking effortlessly fabulous. In downtown Atlanta, "I noticed everyone dressed up," Sara said, "whether they were working in offices or . . . shopping or having lunch with their friends." On the street, she noticed, "All of the women looked so cute, wearing pretty colorful dresses or little capri pants and high heels." She said she wanted to look like she fit in—thus the white pants. And they didn't just look great on the hanger; every time she put them on, they fit her perfectly. They fit the bill for "effortlessly fabulous"—in every way but the one that counted.[1]

The problem with the pants—in a nutshell—was the rear view. Sara believed they looked amazing everywhere *except* on her rear. The issue was that she could not figure out what to wear *under* them. Regular underwear definitely didn't work—the panty lines were lumpy and clearly visible. They drew attention to her backside for all the wrong reasons. She even tried the pants on over a thong a couple times, but she didn't like how they felt. Plus, thong underwear solved *only* the VPL—visible panty line—problem; they didn't help at all with her other issues. "I was terribly frustrated by not having the right undergarment available," she said, "so I could wear those pants with comfort and confidence."

Only a size two at the time, Sara was both tiny and physically fit. Yet she couldn't help noticing what she described as "some cellulite on the back of my thighs that you could see through the pants."[2] The curve-hugging trousers, both white and thin, made every bump and ripple stand out. That was not confidence-building.

With the party only weeks away, she stood paralyzed in front of her closet. For the anticipated warm summer evening, she'd already settled on a beautiful blouse and her favorite pair of high-heeled sandals. As she considered the bottom half of the outfit, her thoughts kept going back to the white pants. A good mix of businesslike and fashionable, they would project self-confidence and style.

## The Shapewear Problem

Sara finally made a decision. This time, she was not going to put the trousers back on the hanger and try to find something else. She was going to wear the damn pants. This called for an undergarment expert.

Taking the pants with her, Sara started visiting local department stores. At each store, after weaving her way through racks to the beige back corner, she explained her problem to a lingerie salesperson. She soon learned that the solution was "shapewear," which she'd never even heard of. But the clerk eagerly pulled several items off the shapewear rack, plopped the stack into her arms, and guided her to the dressing room. Willing to try anything, Sara gamely tried them on.

"When I put on the leggings they suggested, they were so thick," she noted. Plus, she said they "provided more control than I actually needed, which made them extremely uncomfortable." Instead of creating a smooth look under the pants, these undergarments actually created more lumps. Wherever the elastic components had been stitched together, the seams showed clearly through the pants. And even the smoothest underpants dug into her skin at the waist and along their bottom edge, creating ugly "dents" with bulges above and below.

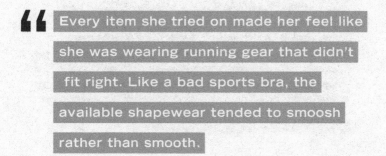

Every item she tried on made her feel like she was wearing running gear that didn't fit right. Like a bad sports bra, the available shapewear tended to smoosh rather than smooth.

"Those leggings weren't solving my issue. If anything, it made things worse," Sara said.[3]

And she knew right away that she could forget about feeling comfortable in any of them. Every item she tried on made her feel like she was wearing running gear that didn't fit right.[4] Like a bad sports bra, the available shapewear tended to smoosh rather than smooth.

Sara left every store empty-handed. Everything she had found was uncomfortable and totally inadequate. Then it suddenly occurred to her: pantyhose might be a great solution. She knew from experience that a good pair of control-tops would certainly smooth and shape her thighs and rear. And because she could wear them as her only undergarments, she'd have no VPLs.

Back at home, she tried on the whole outfit with pantyhose under the pants, and she was right. She felt and looked amazing—until she looked at her feet. With the hosiery seam obvious on her toes and peeking out of the sandals, she looked like somebody's grandma.

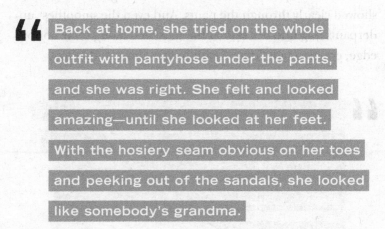

Back at home, she tried on the whole outfit with pantyhose under the pants, and she was right. She felt and looked amazing—until she looked at her feet. With the hosiery seam obvious on her toes and peeking out of the sandals, she looked like somebody's grandma.

Like most working women in the late 1990s, Sara was familiar with the shortcomings of pantyhose. After all, women at the time were expected to wear pantyhose all day, every day. Many employers spelled out the pantyhose requirement in office dress codes. Women in the southern United States dealt with the heat, itchiness, and overall discomfort of pantyhose at least seven months of the year. For Sara, the only loophole she discovered for skipping pantyhose was when she wore trousers. Only then could she wear sandals without a pantyhose seam.

The day of the party inevitably arrived. Out of other ideas by this point, Sara did the only thing she could think of. She cut the feet off her control-top pantyhose, enabling her to wear what was left of them out of sight under the long pants. And it worked! She felt completely confident and comfortable in the pants. "I looked fabulous, I felt great, I had no panty lines, I looked thinner and smoother," she later said. "I remember thinking, 'This should exist for women.'"[5]

She had no way of knowing that she had just come up with an idea that would change the world, one bottom at a time, and in a few years, make her America's youngest female self-made billionaire.[6]

■ **LESSON WE CAN LEARN FROM THE SPANX STORY: DON'T OVERLOOK YOUR OPPORTUNITY**

What common problem, obstacle, or annoyance in your daily life can lead you to a breakthrough idea? What are you stepping over that you could or should be turning into a stepping-stone for your success? Open your eyes and look for your opportunity.

"For every failure, there's an alternative course of action. You just have to find it. When you come to a roadblock, take a detour."

—MARY KAY ASH,
Entrepreneur and Founder of Mary Kay Cosmetics

CHAPTER TWO

# AN UNLIKELY ENTREPRENEUR

The billion-dollar question is, *Why, Sara?* She wore her invention to that party in 1998, but after it was over, why didn't she go back to her apartment, toss the ruined pantyhose in the garbage, go to bed, wake up the next morning, and get on with her life? Cutting the feet out of pantyhose wasn't groundbreaking. It wasn't even that unusual. Women had been doing it for years. What did she see in the idea that no one else had before her? And once she recognized the idea's potential, how was she able to take it from concept to prototype to phenomenon—with no debt and no outside funding? How did she turn her life savings of $5,000 into $1 billion?

The short answer? She was ready. The long one? She had only just arrived at that point. For most of her life, Sara had been trying to get ready for something else entirely—but was thwarted or diverted at every turn.

• • •

> " Once she recognized the idea's potential,
> how was she able to take it from concept
> to prototype to phenomenon—with no debt
> and no outside funding? How did she turn
> her life savings of $5,000 into $1 billion?

## Taking Aim at an Early Age

From the age of eight, Sara Blakely knew exactly what she wanted to do when she grew up: she was going to be a lawyer, just like her dad. While other children progressed through career dreams that might include "fairy princess" or "movie star" or "firefighter," Sara stuck with hers throughout her childhood.

In their hometown of Clearwater Beach, Florida, Sara's father was a prominent trial attorney. She said that from the time she and her brother were little, he often told them fascinating stories at the dinner table about his day in court or at the office. Soon, Sara was dreaming of following in his footsteps. Her dad encouraged her, even allowing her to skip class in elementary school from time to time so that she could join him in the courtroom to hear his closing arguments.

"Becoming a lawyer was a rite of passage in my family," Sara said. She didn't just find entertainment in her dad's closing arguments and stories. She liked the law itself.[1] A child full of curiosity from a young age, she absorbed what her father taught her and went looking for more. From elementary school through high school, many of her school activities were based on whether they would bring her closer to her goal of becoming an attorney.

## On a Different Course during Her Free Time

Sara was like her dad in many ways. She was friendly and articulate. She showed leadership and the ability to motivate. Her plan to follow in his footsteps made a lot of sense. But Sara also took after her mom, and that led her on a parallel path. Mom was a watercolor artist, and Sara not only watched her paint all the time; she inherited some of her mother's creativity and talent.

"I'm what happens when those two mate," she said.[2] Growing up, Sara enjoyed drawing pictures. She created charms and sewed them on socks. She even created and wrote a newspaper. But unlike many artistic kids, she combined her creativity with a desire—and ability—to make a buck. Her sketches didn't just go up on the family refrigerator; one of her earliest memories was drawing and selling pictures door-to-door with a friend on a rainy day.[3] She wore her socks with sewn-on charms to school and her classmates loved them, so she started taking orders and selling them. Soon, a charm sock trend was sweeping the school.[4] That's right, Spanx wasn't the first new clothing genre Sara designed.

Sara took her moneymaking a step beyond selling art. She discovered that she really enjoyed starting all kinds of little businesses. "Thinking of ways to make money has always been a game to me," she said.[5] She had early success charging her friends an admission fee when they came over to roller blade in her driveway. She also transformed her yard into a miniature golf course and her home into a Halloween haunted house (for which she charged admission, of course). And when she had chores to do, like pulling weeds, she often managed to convince her friends to help with her work, Tom Sawyer style, by turning the chores into competitions.[6]

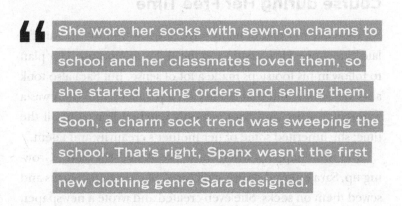

> She wore her socks with sewn-on charms to school and her classmates loved them, so she started taking orders and selling them. Soon, a charm sock trend was sweeping the school. That's right, Spanx wasn't the first new clothing genre Sara designed.

## Failure Is the Only Good Option

Throughout her childhood, Sara continued to be inspired by both of her parents. She said she discovered and developed many creative talents through her mother's help and example. Her father continued to encourage and guide her in preparing for a law career. In high school, she honed her speaking skills on the debate team. But before that, when she was very young, her father had begun teaching her something that increased not only her skills but also her creativity: he celebrated failure.

Sara's dad set up an unusual routine of asking Sara and her brother, Ford, about their failures at the dinner table. After they sat down to eat, he would start the conversation with the question, "What did you fail at this week?" Whether they described a sports tryout where they didn't make the team, or a new unit in math that they were struggling with, he never expressed disappointment at their failures or mistakes. Instead, he acted pleased about every failure, offering them a high five and exclaiming, "Great job!" He only acted disappointed when they had no failure to share, so it soon became clear that failure was something he wanted to hear about. The more things they tried but didn't succeed at, the more their dad celebrated with them. And he always pressed them to tell the whole story about the attempt and the failure. And after they told it, he again said how proud he was of them.

Early on, the children learned to come to the table with at least one failure to talk about. To be able to do this, they constantly sought challenges to try and fail at. All of those frequent unsuccessful attempts, and the dinnertime conversations that followed, gradually led to a reframing of failure in their minds. "My dad taught me that failure is not an outcome," Sara said. Instead, she learned from him that failure should be defined as a lack of trying, or "not stretching yourself far enough out of your comfort zone and attempting to be more than you were the day before."[7]

This unorthodox method had the result of removing the stigma of failure for Sara. Rather than avoiding or even fearing it, Sara and Ford learned to seek it. But their father didn't stop with just a high five. After every failure story, he would encourage them to use the failure, to learn something from it, to grow in some way—with the goal of becoming more than they were the day before. Sara described how that impacted her: "You would realize like, *Oh well, I didn't make the team, but I met my best friend in tryouts.* There was just always something there that made it worth doing."[8] From her father's teaching on growing through failure, Sara learned to believe in the possibility of finding a positive in the negative.

## But Sometimes It Takes
## Longer Than a Dinner Conversation

Of course, not all negative experiences are the result of our own attempts and failures. Many things happen to us in life that are completely outside of our control. Some, like a major loss or tragedy, add grief and helplessness into the mix of negative emotions. Mourning and processing the injustice of it all takes time. Choosing to reframe and move past a failed math test can be challenging. When tragedy hits, finding something positive within it feels impossible. At only sixteen, Sara Blakely experienced that kind of tragedy.

On a sunny afternoon, Sara was out riding her bicycle with her best friend, Susie, in their quiet neighborhood. Susie was riding in front as they approached a corner and began to make their way across. Susie entered the intersection just ahead of Sara, when several things happened at once. Suddenly, a car was there, approaching fast. And as Sara watched in horror, Susie and her bicycle, which had been right in front of her just a moment before, received the full impact of the speeding vehicle. Momentum carried car, bicycle, and girl several yards before coming to a stop. "I saw the whole thing," Sara said. "Her body was lying on the side of the road where it had been dragged. Blood coming out of her ears, nose, her eyes, her mouth. I think I collapsed. People said it would be OK but I knew it wasn't OK."[9]

As she described it years later, "Grief has knocked me to my knees. There have been some very dark moments."[10] Like many people who have lost a loved one, Sara pondered the fragility of life and the inevitability of death. "I think that when you witness death at age 16, there's a sense of urgency about life," she said years later. "The thought of my mortality—I think about it a lot. I find it motivating. It can be any time that your number's up."[11]

Grief took its course. And even with her father's constant exhortations to find a lesson in every failure, it was difficult to find a silver lining in a cloud this dark. Over time, however, an idea slowly emerged: no amount of grief could change the past. But maybe, if Sara focused on gratitude and lived her own life to the fullest, she could honor Susie's memory. Processing this idea would take many years, but eventually Sara concluded that her best response to losing loved ones was to live "for the people who didn't get a chance to." She said this reminder—that life is temporary—freed her in a way. After experiencing the finality of loss, nothing else seemed to matter as much.[12]

## Finding Hope in an Unlikely Place

Not long after Susie's death, Sara's high school career was marked by one more loss—less permanent than death but no less tragic for a teenager. One day, Sara's father walked into her room and broke the news to her that he would be moving out soon. He and her mother were separating and would soon divorce. Sara's daily life was about to go through a drastic change.

Soon, Sara's dad was packing to move out. He walked in to Sara's room with a box and set it before her. Inside were two rows of cassette tapes, nestled in molded plastic. And the lid read: *"How to Be a No-Limit Person, by Wayne Dyer."* Sara's dad explained, "I'm giving this to you right now because I wish someone had given it to me when I was your age." He didn't learn the lessons on those tapes until he was in his forties. But then they changed his life, he said. "And I think they can change yours." According to Sara, that statement "left an indelible mark."[13] And that was why she decided to give the tapes a listen.

Wayne Dyer was a popular inspirational speaker referred to as "the father of motivation." Listening to him, she understood the appeal. He *was* motivational. And inspiring. She was soon hooked. Every day, driving in her car back and forth to school, she carried that box of tapes. On the cassette player, she listened again and again to the entire course. She said she learned about the power of visualization along with clear and concrete lessons on the value of setting goals. Most interesting to her was the lesson on the positive results that can come from simply picturing outcomes. Through *How to Be a No-Limit Person*, she found solace and discovered possibilities.

"I listened to the series over and over until I had all ten tapes memorized," she said.[14] Sara said she learned as she kept listening to the course how to stop caring so much about what other people thought. This ended up serving her especially well as she finished high school, because her friends refused to ride in her car with her. "It became a running joke among my friends that nobody wanted to end up in my car because they would have to listen to the motivational tapes," she said, laughing many years later. "Fast-forward all these years later, and I get on the cover of *Forbes*," she said, referring to the March 26, 2012, edition. "My friends from high school texted me and all they wrote was, 'I should have listened to those tapes.'"[15]

## A Unique Summer Job

Sara graduated from high school and had been accepted by Florida State University—her next step toward law school. But that summer before heading off to Tallahassee, she was on the lookout for new ways to earn money. She looked around her tourist community, which had several beachfront hotels and resorts. Hanging out on the beach next to the huge Hilton resort, she could see the hotel's guests, many of them families with young children. She designed and printed fliers for a daytime "kids' club" at the Hilton, offering to entertain and care for little ones on the beach for $8 per child. Parents eagerly took her up on the offer, and the business soon became a huge success. She later said she made more money during the two-month summer season than her friends did at their "traditional" jobs over the course of a year.[16]

For three summers, Sara worked for herself, hanging out on the beach in her bathing suit, entertaining kids for a few hours each day while their parents relaxed. After all that success, she was eager to expand her business by offering her services to guests at other hotels and resorts. Her first step, she decided, was to discuss her idea with the Hilton general manager.

But on the day that Sara met with the manager of the Hilton, things did not go at all as expected. After she shared her pitch for an expansion of her babysitting program, it became clear that the manager had no idea who she was, *and* that this did not make him happy. She did not have CPR training, insurance, or permission to be there. And now he was learning that this petite, ponytailed *kid* had spent the past three summers—starting when she was still a minor!—running her own business out of his hotel? Even worse, the Hilton *already had* its own official babysitting program, so Sara's kids' club had actually stolen some of their business. As she described it, "He literally escorted me off the premises."[17]

That day, after the manager himself walked Sara to the edge of the Hilton resort property and told her never to set foot there again, her babysitting business was no more. Of course, it could have been much worse. She was very, very fortunate. What if a child *had* gotten hurt? Or lost? She was lucky she didn't get sued. Or arrested. Years later, it would become one more of her failure stories, told often in interviews. Once again, Sara had learned something—in this case, several things *not* to do. Her kids' club debacle would turn out to be one of her first business lessons.[18]

## Back to School

That summer soon came to an end, and the failure was tempered by the progress Sara was making toward her bachelor's degree at Florida State University. She continued sharpening her rhetorical skills on the debate team, along with leading cheers at football games. Majoring in legal communication, she was still on track in pursuit of her goal.

Sara's senior year arrived, and she prepared to take the LSAT exam, which was required for admission into law school. And after a childhood spent learning from her trial lawyer dad, and then studying legal communication at the university, she had done everything she could to prepare for law school. The only thing between her and acceptance into a graduate law program, followed by a successful career in law, was the correct score on the LSAT.

## The Last Undergrad Hurdle

The day came that fall for the LSAT placement exam. Sara knew how to prepare herself, but she would be striving to overcome something that was not in her power: Sara was a poor test taker. She admitted that her reading comprehension was "not great." Plus, she said, "I have trouble focusing for long periods of time." Had the years of listening to Wayne Dyer's teaching developed her "positive thinker" side well enough to give her a passing grade?

In a room packed with other aspiring lawyers, Sara took the test. Afterward, all she could do was wait several weeks until scores were released. Unfortunately, the number printed on the letter indicated that the "poor test taker" within her had triumphed. She had not earned a high enough score to qualify for law school. Or, as she put it, "I did *horribly.*"[19]

This was discouraging news, but Sara's response was what might be expected from her. She refused to give up. She said, "I scraped myself up off the floor, enrolled in an LSAT prep course, studied my ass off, and took the test again."[20] That's what she had been trained to do by her father, after all: to welcome failure and learn from it.

So Sara studied hard, earned a fantastic score, got accepted by Harvard Law, and the rest is history, right? Wrong. She failed again. She later admitted that, in fact, "I did one point worse."[21] After the second failure, Sara found herself, at age twenty-two, with no idea what to do next. "*What is the universe trying to tell me?*" she wondered.[22] She had been pursuing a career in law for more than half her life. She now had a bachelor's degree, but no way forward.

■ **LESSON WE CAN LEARN FROM THE SPANX STORY: FIND THE GIFT IN FAILURE**

Sara Blakely once said, "Every terrible thing that happens to you always has a hidden gift and is leading you to something greater. I actually started writing them in my

> notebook." She continued, "I log and keep track of all the
> terrible things that happened to me, because it's almost
> become a game for me now. I like to see the gift when it
> unfolds."[23] Do you believe there is a potential gift hidden
> in every failure, mistake, or difficulty? Decide to look for
> it. How can you find the gift in a current difficulty you're
> facing?

## What Are You Going to Do Next?

You may remember a clever marketing campaign that started
back in the late 1980s that has continued for more than three
decades. A commercial shows the MVP of the NFL Super Bowl
walking off of the football field just minutes after winning the
game, and he's asked, "You've just won the Super Bowl—what
are you going to do next?" He looks at the camera and shouts,
"I'm going to Disney World!"

Based on Sara's two failing LSAT scores, she was not the
winner of anything—much less a championship football game.
Yet, she decided to do what a Super Bowl victor would do. "In
my mind," she said, "the universe was now telling me to drive
to Disney World." Not to celebrate, but to look for a job. "I had
dedicated the past fifteen years of my life to school, participat-
ing in debate clubs in high school and college and watching my
dad excel as a lawyer, believing this would be my path, too. It
was shocking to realize this wasn't going to be my life. I was so
devastated that I hadn't done well on my LSAT that I wanted to
escape reality a little longer after college before figuring out
what I would do."[24]

Her plan B: drive from her home in Clearwater Beach to
Walt Disney World in Orlando. There, she would audition to

play the costumed character Goofy in the amusement park. "Something about being Goofy felt right," she said. The added bonus was that "at least no one would know it was me inside the costume."[25]

But that plan failed, too. First, once at Disney, Sara was told that as a new "cast member" (the name Disney used for all employees), she would be required to work in the park for at least three months before even being considered for a costumed character role. And, to pile on the disappointment, she learned that to play Goofy, an employee had to be at least six feet tall. Sara is five foot six. They told her she might qualify to play a chipmunk.[26]

Because she had no plan C, Sara accepted the only job Disney offered her. And within a week, she was convinced that Disney was a fabulous corporation. "Working at Disney World was a pleasant enough experience for the few months I was there," she said. "But the truth is, I was bored. And I was unhappy."[27] She spent her work hours wearing a brown polyester uniform, buckling guest after guest into a ride at Epcot. It took no time at all for her to get disillusioned. She said, "My first day at Disney I went on break and saw Snow White dragging on a cigarette."[28]

Sara's work wasn't exactly fulfilling, either. "I had to walk on a moving sidewalk for eight hours a day and say, 'Hi, welcome to Disney, watch your step, please.'" Her face clearly visible every day, she found herself face-to-face with school friends who would "look at my big Mickey Mouse name tag, and be like, 'Sara? Sara Blakely? Is that you?' I'd sheepishly say, 'Yeah, just get on the ride.'"[29]

Before she could even fulfill her three-month commitment and audition to wear a character costume, Sara concluded that her plan to escape reality at Disney had backfired. "I'd had my fill of 'the happiest place on earth,'" she said, "and decided to return home and live with my mom."[30]

## Time to Regroup and Rethink Everything

A lot of people would have been crushed by a series of situations like these. But Wayne Dyer's teaching on positivity and her father's teaching on failure were still speaking to Sara. If law school wasn't for her, then she would look ahead and find a new path. In her case, the next step in her journey was revealed when she literally looked up.

> **If law school wasn't for her, then she would look ahead and find a new path.**

One day back in Clearwater, while driving through town, Sara saw above her a billboard advertising a job in sales at Danka, a company based right there in Florida.[31] Later acquired by Konica Minolta in the United States, Danka was an international company, worth $1 billion at the time. They were primarily in the office machine business, selling printers, copiers, and fax machines. A job with Danka, selling fax machines to local businesses, could be a step in a good direction. Sara was friendly, outgoing, and down-to-earth. People seemed to naturally like her. And from charging admission to skate in her driveway to building a thriving (but unsanctioned) hotel beach babysitting program all by herself, she already had years of practice in connecting with others and selling. Her résumé could also include communication skills sharpened on the college debate team. Even the few miserable months at Walt Disney World had given her valuable customer service experience. Applying at Danka made sense, at least for the time being.

## Cold Calls

Sara took the plunge. She applied for—and got—her first "real" job out of college. Soon after Danka hired her, she was excelling at her role. But as Sara remembered it, the company expected *a lot* without offering a lot of help. "They gave me a cubicle, a phone book and a territory of four zip codes in Clearwater and said, 'now go sell $20,000 of fax machines a month door-to-door,'" she recalled.[32]

Yet, Sara accepted the daunting challenge. Confident that success came in the trying and growing, she learned—from rejection after rejection—how to sell as successfully as possible in the most challenging of environments. "I had to 100 percent drum up my own leads," she said. She cold-called potential customers on the phone and walked up to offices without an invitation. "I would wake up in the morning and drive around cold calling from eight until five," she said, lugging heavy fax machines around in the Florida heat. Many people hung up on her and "most doors were slammed in my face." It wasn't uncommon for an office manager to tear up her business card and throw it at her. She even had a few police escorts out of buildings.

Yet Sara soldiered on. "It wasn't long before I grew immune to the word 'no' and even found my situation amusing," she said, learning that she was capable of finding humor in almost anything.[33] Pressing on after all the "no" answers, Sara developed even more determination and charm. And she did make a lot of sales. Unfortunately, almost every sale to a company was a one-off. Once an office had a fax machine, they didn't usually need to buy another one.

It may come as no shock that the Danka job had very high turnover. In fact, Sara said, "It was the kind of place that would hire anyone with a pulse."[34] And most people lasted no more than a month or two. But Sara stuck it out. She managed to connect with even the most resistant customers and meet her sales quota. It also didn't hurt that she was quick to recognize and admit when she had made a mistake or had done something completely absentminded. She had no problem laughing at herself. One day while already out on sales calls, she suddenly realized that she was wearing two completely different-colored shoes: one black and the other a vibrant royal blue. But rather than rushing home to change shoes, she decided to laugh it off and let potential clients in on the joke. It worked. She got her *mismatched* feet in more doors than usual that day. "It was such a good way to open doors. People didn't kick me out of offices, because I'd say, 'Yep, look what I did today.' There's just so much lesson in that as far as being willing to laugh at yourself. It humanizes you. It's the best way to connect with people."[35] She made note of what she discovered: people were willing to give a chance to someone who was authentic and open.

Rejection also became Sara's teacher. Rather than letting it discourage her, she used it as motivation to keep pressing on, day after day, month after month. Eventually, year after year. "I learned that no doesn't always mean no," she said. "And that you may get thirty nos before you get the one yes."[36] That was a realization that would serve her well in the future.

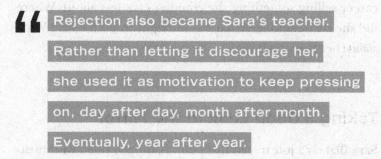

" Rejection also became Sara's teacher. Rather than letting it discourage her, she used it as motivation to keep pressing on, day after day, month after month. Eventually, year after year.

## Settling in at Danka . . . Or Just Settling?

Because she never gave up and never stopped learning in a job that would have crushed most people, Sara thrived at Danka. It didn't take long for her increasing sales numbers to impress her bosses. As she met and then exceeded their expectations, she began to advance. When she was twenty-five, her skill in selling door-to-door had so impressed them that she was promoted to be the company's national sales trainer. Based in Atlanta, she would do seminars all over the United States instructing Danka salespeople in door-to-door sales.[37]

For Sara, selling fax machines, and then training others to do so, was a lucrative job that she did very well. Her passion wasn't in this kind of sales job, however. "I didn't enjoy selling fax machines," she said. However, she liked "dealing with people and selling them something they needed—even if they didn't know it yet."[38]

It was clear that Sara was nowhere close to where she had imagined herself to be. "One day, I pulled off the side of the road," Sara said, "and I literally thought, 'I'm in the wrong movie.'"[39] Her attempt to get paid to be goofy, by literally *being Goofy*, had failed. Now, she was a few years into a successful career selling something she couldn't care less about. Where did she really belong? What was the right "role" for her? What *should* her story really be?

## Taking a Good Look in the Mirror

Sara Blakely's journey to this point had been filled with twists and turns and detours, veering away from much of what she thought she wanted. But those detours had a profound effect on Sara: she and her desires had changed. So she got out a notebook and started writing.

"I recognized that one of my strengths was selling. I really enjoyed it and knew I was good at it."[40] But it was also clear to her that she wouldn't feel fulfilled until she was self-employed, selling a product or service that she was passionate about. And that wasn't fax machines. And even more ideal? To sell a product that she herself had created. On that day, the right "movie" came into focus. In her journal, she wrote, "I want to invent or create a product that I can sell that's my own and not somebody else's, and I want it to be something I can sell to millions of people. And I want it to be something that makes people feel good."[41]

## Set Goals—Be Open

According to everything Sara had been taught, there was power in what she'd written in her journal to create a positive outcome. "I became very specific with my visualizations,"[42] she said, channeling that positive expectation into a daily search for *her* big idea: a product she could invent. Every day while driving to work in Atlanta traffic, she would say to herself, "I want my idea; I'm ready for it."[43]

> ### ▓ LESSON WE CAN LEARN FROM THE SPANX STORY: TRUST YOUR GUT
>
> **For an opportunity to be right for you, it needs to match who you are. "Go within yourself and ask what makes sense," Sara Blakely often said. "Listen to your own gut instincts and map out a sensible strategy. Don't worry so much about what other people know or think they know."[44] Like Sara, you can get better at understanding your instincts. Learn to recognize which intuitive ideas and feelings could take you in the right direction, and begin listening to them more.**

LinkedIn founder Reid Hoffman observed in a *Masters of Scale* podcast that featured Sara, "She had spent years scanning the horizon for that neon sign pointing to her big idea."[45] Sara was prepared to go for whatever idea presented itself. So when her "neon sign" lit up, she was ready.

By the time Sara received the invitation to the party, she was on "high alert."[46] And then the day of the party, when she found a solution to the problem with her pants, she took notice. According to Hoffman, "All the other women who had the same thought simply went to their party and back to work the next morning, leaving the neon sign 'This should exist' behind them in the night." He explained that this is a myth about entrepreneurship: "that big ideas drop out of the sky, land in your lap, and transform you into a billionaire the next day. Ta-da! This almost never happens. Yes, Sara did have a key moment of inspiration in her bedroom getting ready for a party, and that matters." But, he pointed out, she "had already oriented herself squarely in the direction of a big idea."[47]

For Sara Blakely, the invention of Spanx was no accident or coincidence. She had spent twenty-seven years getting ready for this specific moment. When she failed the LSAT, she wasn't able to see where her new path would lead. "I'm a horrible test taker, thank God, because life had other plans for me," she said. "Spanx would not exist if I did great on the LSAT."[48] Even throughout her childhood and education, while she thought she was pursuing a law degree, she was actually learning critical skills for this new venture that she didn't know she would need, such as how to fail, how to sell, and how to think creatively.

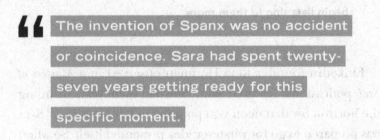

> The invention of Spanx was no accident or coincidence. Sara had spent twenty-seven years getting ready for this specific moment.

Author and financial expert Wes Moss wrote about Sara's epiphany after the party: "For some women, the undergarment solution was just a way to finish off an outfit. For Sara, it was a sign from the universe."[49] She had experienced the moment. She had found her idea. The door was open. Could she walk through it? Could she figure out how to take a good idea and make it into something real?

## LESSON WE CAN LEARN FROM THE SPANX STORY: DON'T LET OTHERS WRITE YOUR SCRIPT

Sara paid attention and realized that she was "in the wrong movie." What about you? Are you in the right movie? Have you taken an inventory of your strengths and weaknesses? Do you know what you really want, what would bring out the best in you? What experiences in your life, both positive and negative, have prepared you for your purpose?

"A brilliant idea doesn't guarantee a successful invention. Real magic comes from a brilliant idea combined with willpower, tenacity, and a willingness to make mistakes."

—LORI GREINER,
Inventor and *Shark Tank* Panelist

## CHAPTER THREE

# A LESS LIKELY PRODUCT

If the modified pantyhose Sara wore to that party in Atlanta in 1998 had worked perfectly, Spanx might not exist today. Fortunately for women's bodies all over the world, it was immediately obvious to her that the DIY footless pantyhose was an imperfect solution. Sara actually felt pretty annoyed with them several times during the evening. "I looked fabulous, I felt great, I had no panty lines, I looked thinner and smoother," she said. "But they rolled up my legs all night."[1] That one problem actually confirmed in her mind that this might be her big idea. No one else was selling footless pantyhose that didn't roll up. Taking scissors to a new pair every time she went out wasn't practical because of the annoyance factor—and the cost. "I remember thinking, 'I've got to figure out how to make this,'" she said. *I just needed an undergarment that didn't exist.*[2]

Sara knew this was a good idea. It had the potential to fill a gap in the market between ordinary underwear and ugly, restrictive girdles, but she didn't know how to start creating it as a product. As a legal communications major in college, she'd never taken a single business class. And yet, in spite of her lack of knowledge and education in the "right" ways to pursue her dream, Sara could draw upon her twenty-seven years of life experience and lessons: She was good at solving problems and making things happen within her means. She was a hard worker and unafraid of failure. She was skilled in connecting with people and opening doors. And she was convinced that she could sell something she believed in.

Sara intuitively knew she needed to think big, yet start small, she said. "A lot of people want to start big and think big and oftentimes get ahead of themselves," she explained. "That can end wildly successful, but it can also cause a lot of problems."[3] By starting small on her big idea, she could make continuous progress but not overextend herself or her resources. At this early stage, Sara didn't quit her job, or go looking for outside investors, or go into debt. She was committed to working with the resources (time and money) that she had available to her.

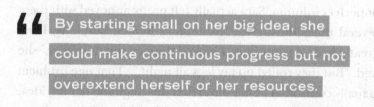

" By starting small on her big idea, she could make continuous progress but not overextend herself or her resources.

As for available money, Sara had a savings account containing $5,000, which she'd been setting aside for months for her future invention. Money she'd previously earned selling fax machines would be used to create what she needed to pitch to retailers. As for available time, she continued the pattern she'd set before her "neon sign" lit up, searching for it whenever she was free. Now she would just continue that pattern: working on her invention on nights and weekends. After all, her day job was providing ongoing income and benefits. Even though it would limit the time available to work on her idea, she kept the nine-to-five job at Danka.

## Shhh! It's a Secret!

Sara's next decision might come as a surprise: as she started pursuing the idea, she chose not to run it by any of her friends or family. "For the first full year I kept my idea a secret from anyone who could not directly help to move it forward," she said. "That was my gut instinct at the time."[4] She let them know she was working on something, but she wouldn't tell them what it was. Because they knew and loved her, they didn't press for more information. Most of her loved ones simply shrugged, telling each other, "Sara's working on some crazy idea."[5]

Why did she choose not to share with the people closest to her? She later said, "That one felt very specific and different to me. So I didn't ask anybody or tell anybody about it." In her opinion, it is one of the main reasons Spanx exists today. "I believe that ideas are the most vulnerable in their infancy," she explained.[6]

In the early days after someone comes up with an idea, it's fragile. And yet that's when many people want to run it by friends or family, saying they just want to be sure it isn't crazy. But this search for validation often backfires. They say things like, "If this is such a great idea, why hasn't anyone invented it before now?" Or, "Even if you do create it, some big company will make something similar and crush you in competition." Sara sensed that sharing this idea wouldn't be wise at first. "I just intuitively did not want to invite ego into the process too soon. Once the idea had arrived in my life, I wanted to spend the time pursuing it and not defending it and explaining it."[7]

## LESSON WE CAN LEARN FROM THE SPANX STORY: VALUE PERSPIRATION OVER VALIDATION

When many people get an idea, the first thing they want to do is run it by friends and family to receive validation. Instead, Sara trusted her instincts, kept it to herself, and got to work. "I worked on Spanx until I had enough of myself invested that I wouldn't turn back regardless of what I heard," she said years later. "I'm pretty positive that if I had told my friends and family about Spanx early on I'd still be selling fax machines."[8] If you have an idea, don't put yourself in a place where others can talk you out of it. Focus on what you can do to move so far forward in the process that the comments of others can't discourage you.

## First Step

Sara's first step during her year of secret work was to try to get a patent on the product, since she wanted to protect her invention. Because she had no idea how to do that, she just pulled out the local phone book and began calling patent attorneys. She said she really wanted a female patent attorney, because "I thought it would be much easier to explain my idea [for a women's product]" to another woman. But at the time, there were no female patent attorneys in the entire state of Georgia. It would be more difficult to help male attorneys understand the concept, but she had no choice.[9]

Sara soon found three firms that she liked and made appointments to see them in person. At each meeting, the attorney asked her to describe her invention. Still very excited about discovering her big idea, she did her best to explain how it was going to *change the world* by making *women's butts look better,* and everyone would love it. But each time, after she stopped talking, she was greeted with blank stares. In fact, one attorney started suspiciously peering around the room. He later admitted to Sara that her idea had sounded so bad to him that, "I thought you had been sent by Candid Camera."[10]

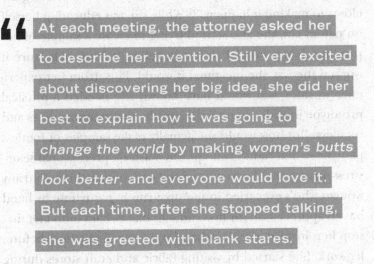

> At each meeting, the attorney asked her to describe her invention. Still very excited about discovering her big idea, she did her best to explain how it was going to *change the world* by making *women's butts look better,* and everyone would love it. But each time, after she stopped talking, she was greeted with blank stares.

Even though the attorneys were skeptical, each one quoted a price to write and submit a patent application. That was when it became clear that the services of a patent attorney weren't cheap. One asked for $5,000. The cheapest was $3,000.

Working with an attorney, the patenting process alone could eat up all of her money. Since that wasn't an option, what could she do? She decided to write the patent application herself. How hard could it be? She visited her local Barnes & Noble bookstore and bought a book on patents and trademarks. At night she began studying the complicated process of applying for a patent all on her own.

## Testing Her Idea

"I didn't know what I was doing," Sara said. "But I focused on getting at least one thing done each day that would bring me closer to making it happen."[11] While she was educating herself on patent law, she also started trying to create a sample of her product. It was crucial to test it, refine it, and make sure it worked the way she imagined it would. Plus, from her experience in sales, she would have known she needed a physical prototype in order to pitch the product to manufacturers and retailers. But how would she actually make samples of footless pantyhose that didn't roll up? She wasn't a professional seamstress; in fact, she'd never even used a sewing machine. And any woman who's ever tried to sew up a run in pantyhose by hand has an appreciation for how difficult that is. Sara didn't let that stop her; instead, she did what she'd done many times before: legwork. She started by visiting fabric and craft stores during her off hours and weekends, with the existing cutoff pantyhose in hand. She'd buy small strips of different types of elastic and lace off the shelf. And use paper clips to attach them to the bottom edge of the pantyhose.

Sara's Frankenstein-ish pantyhose creations made it very clear, very quickly, that she did not have the skills to sew or assemble a viable sample on her own. In fact, it would be impossible for anyone to create what she was imagining on a home sewing machine, even as a prototype. Her footless pantyhose invention absolutely needed specialized machinery. She just needed a manufacturer who already had the right machines.[12]

Once again, she discovered a subject that she needed to learn more about before proceeding. How *were* pantyhose made, anyway? Who were the experienced manufacturers? She got on a computer and searched on the internet.[13] After some clicking around, she concluded that the majority of hosiery manufacturers seemed to be located in North Carolina, just a state away. She found the contact information for each mill. Now she was ready to ask for their help in creating her prototype.

## But First, Another Visit to the Bookstore

Months had gone by at this point, as Sara kept working at her day job while creating her patent application at night. Still without a patent, she wanted to make sure her invention idea wouldn't be stolen after she shared it with the manufacturers. So, this time, she went out and bought a book on inventions. Reading through it, she soon learned that the legal way to keep a secret in the business world is called a nondisclosure agreement (NDA).[14] Since Sara was still not willing to ask an attorney to help write it (the "normal" way to obtain an NDA), she just studied the book's sample and wrote one up on her own. Next, she wrote a letter of introduction, describing her footless pantyhose garment and asking for a quote to create a prototype. Along with her NDA, she sent the letter to fifteen different hosiery mills.

## An Unwelcome Pitch
## for an Unlikely Product

Possibly unbeknownst to Sara, she was pitching to an industry in sharp decline. A new generation had entered the work-force—young women who didn't remember a time when skirts and stockings and pumps were required at work, and slacks were forbidden.[15] While women in their thirties and up still might have felt uncomfortable and conspicuous going out without pantyhose, these younger women preferred not to wear them and pushed for change. Plus, while the $5–$10 average that women spent per pair had once been accepted as a neces-sary expenditure, women were beginning to see it as an ex-pense that could be eliminated. As a result, sheer hosiery sales had been falling steadily since 1995.[16] Women weren't buying as many pairs of pantyhose, so hosiery companies weren't or-dering as many from the manufacturers. With the decline, it was practically unheard of to launch a new hosiery brand.[17] And the mills that Sara wrote to were struggling and not eager to take new risks.

Most responded to her written queries, but they were bru-tally honest. Every single response said the idea was stupid or didn't make sense. Probably because all the respondents were male, and thus didn't really get it. They couldn't see how her product was revolutionary or would sell at all. They were also concerned that Sara didn't have any backers. No one was inter-ested in pausing production and losing money to create a small run for a twenty-seven-year-old woman with $5,000 and an idea they were sure wouldn't work.[18]

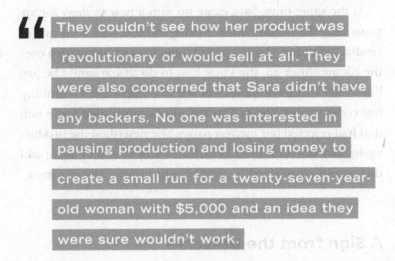

> They couldn't see how her product was revolutionary or would sell at all. They were also concerned that Sara didn't have any backers. No one was interested in pausing production and losing money to create a small run for a twenty-seven-year-old woman with $5,000 and an idea they were sure wouldn't work.

After all her time with Danka, trying to sell fax machines door-to-door, Sara had learned not to take no for an answer. Undeterred, Sara continued her work on the patent application. The most time-consuming (and therefore expensive) part of the application process is the search through every patent ever registered in that category, to make sure no one has patented anything similar. In order to do that, Sara needed to find that list, so she visited the library at Georgia Tech (officially known as the Georgia Institute of Technology). She was in luck! They had a list, and searching through it was a task Sara could do on her own, without even touching her $5,000 budget.

Every evening, after a full day at Danka, Sara could be found in the reference section of the Georgia Tech library. There, she looked up every hosiery patent in existence, all the way back to the 1800s. The search, along with the work of creating as much of the application as she could do herself, took her the better part of a year.[19]

At the same time, Sara came up with a new strategy for approaching the hosiery mills. Writing to them had been unsuccessful. This time, she would call them to explain her idea over the phone. After all, she knew how to do this; it would be just like cold-calling companies to sell fax machines. Consulting her company list, she got on the phone and called every mill that had rejected her idea on paper. She described the product again, and asked for their help. But one by one, they again said they weren't interested in creating a prototype. She was stuck.

## A Sign from the Universe

At this point, Sara had to face the possibility that this wasn't the right path. After about two months with no sign, Sara ended up traveling to another city for Danka. She later recounted sitting on the bed in her hotel room one day and turning on the TV to watch *The Oprah Winfrey Show*. She'd been tuned in for only a few minutes when something happened that made her sit up and take notice. Oprah was simply chatting with a guest about tips for looking and feeling good in the latest fashions. Sharing what worked for her to look smooth and line-free under snug trousers, she illustrated by reaching down and pulling up the leg of her own pants. There, on TV, Sara saw the raw edge of a pair of pantyhose on Oprah Winfrey's leg. *Oprah had just shown the world that she cut off the feet of her hose, to eliminate panty lines and smooth everything under her pants.* The raw edge was even rolling up just as Sara had experienced. For Sara, the sign couldn't have been clearer. She decided it was time to maximize her sales skills by traveling to North Carolina and pitching the manufacturers face-to-face.[20]

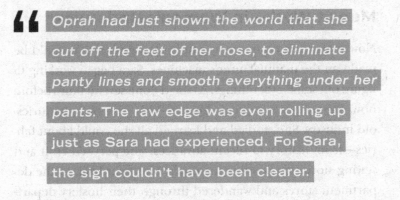

" Oprah had just shown the world that she cut off the feet of her hose, to eliminate panty lines and smooth everything under her pants. The raw edge was even rolling up just as Sara had experienced. For Sara, the sign couldn't have been clearer.

When she got back home to Atlanta from the Danka trip, she had to use her vacation to take a week off of work, but Sara was determined. She was soon back in her car, driving to North Carolina. Over the next seven days, she visited all of the hosiery mills on her list. And . . . every one of them turned her away again. This roadblock was not budging, and she ended up just going home. There was still the patent application to complete, so she went back to working on it during her evenings and weekends.

The two weeks passed. Then one day, Sam Kaplan of Highland Mills, one of the manufacturers Sara had visited in North Carolina, called her.[21] He told her he had changed his mind and decided to help make her prototype. When she asked why, he simply said, "I have two daughters." He had run the idea by them, he explained, and they had surprised him by getting excited about the product and wishing it existed. Assuring him that it was brilliant and made perfect sense, they urged him to "help this girl do it."[22] So now he was calling Sara to offer to make it happen, even though he personally still thought it was crazy. This was the turning point Sara had been waiting for. She immediately said yes. Her product would be one step closer to becoming a reality. It was time to design the prototype.

## Men at Work—in Women's Underwear

Now that it was time to come up with a design that could be made on the manufacturer's machines, Sara began working to figure out some other things. As she'd done several times before now, she set out to educate herself—this time on a centuries-old industry. She studied and learned all she could about fabrics—from history to recent advances. She perused craft and sewing stores for possible materials. She went back to the department stores and wandered through their hosiery departments. Mostly, she visited different hosiery manufacturers, asking questions and taking notes.

One thing Sara said she noticed right away was that the research and development staffs at all the mills were male. "I kept talking to all these men," she said. "And I remember thinking, 'Where are the women? Why am I not speaking to any women here?'" It suddenly dawned on her that this might be the reason why women's hosiery was so uncomfortable: the people designing and making it never had to wear it![23]

The two standard hosiery design and manufacturing practices seemed nonsensical, yet the male designers clung to them. First, while manufacturers traditionally made pantyhose in a wide variety of sizes, for an unexplainable reason the size measurement of the waistbands didn't vary at all. They literally sewed the same-size waistband into every pair of pantyhose, from extra-small to extra-large. This meant that both a ninety-eight-pound woman and a two-hundred-pound woman were expected to wear a pantyhose waistband of exactly the same size. When Sara asked why in the world they would offer a single waist size, which would only be comfortable for a small percentage of women, she was told it was in order to keep production costs low.[24] In other words, in making a decision to save money, the mills had not considered customer comfort *at all.* That meant at least 80 percent of all wearers were in pantyhose that either bound or sagged at the waist.

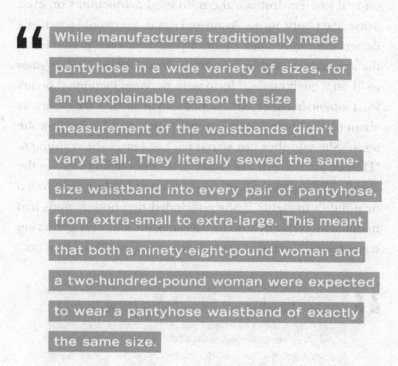

> While manufacturers traditionally made pantyhose in a wide variety of sizes, for an unexplainable reason the size measurement of the waistbands didn't vary at all. They literally sewed the same-size waistband into every pair of pantyhose, from extra-small to extra-large. This meant that both a ninety-eight-pound woman and a two-hundred-pound woman were expected to wear a pantyhose waistband of exactly the same size.

Second, Sara asked about something that has puzzled women for decades: pantyhose size charts. They seem to make absolutely no sense. Many women (and any men who ever had to "pick up a pair" for a significant other) have puzzled over the apparent randomness of size ranges on a package of pantyhose. How could a size B possibly fit one woman measuring 5'1" and 105 pounds, *and* another who was 5'11" and 165—plus everyone in between? And yet, at this writing, that's exactly what the online size chart for Hanes' L'Eggs Sheer Energy Control Top says.[25]

Sara soon learned how the mills measured and "tested" their products, and she said everything began to make sense—in a crazy sort of way. At the time, hosiery was not traditionally tested on real women. Instead, the mills used mannequins or, even worse, flat plastic forms. Again and again, Sara would watch as a design team would put a pair of pantyhose on a plastic form, then stand back and look at how it fit. Pantyhose that *appeared* to fit on a medium-sized form were declared medium.[26] Somewhat tongue-in-cheek, Sara would lean in and ask the designers about the mannequin wearing the pantyhose, "Ask her how she feels." She said they just stared back at her as she continued. "How do you know if this plastic form's not telling you," in the middle of the day, she said, "that it started binding, or it rolled or it didn't fit right?"[27] She concluded that hosiery mills had manufactured pantyhose for decades without ever gathering data on how an actual human being experienced the product.

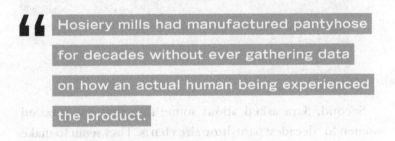

Hosiery mills had manufactured pantyhose for decades without ever gathering data on how an actual human being experienced the product.

## Pardon the Disruption

Sara began detailed conversations with the staff at Sam Kaplan's Highland Mills factory in order to design her prototype. Her ignorance of the inner workings of the hosiery industry back then was a great asset to her—and a huge annoyance for the design team. Coming in as an outsider, she wanted to know *why* they did *everything*. She later said, "I had no idea how it was supposed to be done, and if you have no idea how it's supposed to be done, you will end up being disruptive."[28] She challenged the mill staff at every turn. Instead of accepting fifty-year-old methods or procedures as the "right" ways to do things, she constantly asked if there might be a better way. "I wasn't as intimidated," she later chuckled, "as I should have been."[29]

Working with Highland Mills, Sara's biggest disruption was probably her insistence on focusing on the "wrong" body part. Throughout their history, stockings and then pantyhose had been designed and marketed—by men—as products that would make a woman's legs look attractive primarily to men. The entire product focus was on appearance, because they were meant to be seen on the leg. Then Sara entered the picture and explained her opinion that the product's appearance mattered a whole lot less than its effect *under* a woman's clothing. "An entire industry had been looking at something in one way, and they were on a decline year after year," she said. "I knocked on their door and said, 'guys, I just want your hosiery material, and I don't need it to be seen anywhere. It's actually going to be hidden under clothes. It's a new type of undergarment.'"[30]

## ■ LESSON WE CAN LEARN FROM THE SPANX STORY: ASK QUESTIONS

Sara Blakely put it this way: "I like to tell people what you don't know can be your greatest asset if you let it. If you have the courage." She went on, "You know, a lot of us second guess ourselves and think, well, I didn't go to school for this or I'm not an expert, so we don't ask the questions or we don't pursue it."[31] Use what you don't

> know to make new discoveries, challenge old thinking,
> and introduce innovation.

Still skeptical, Sam eventually did as she asked and put together prototypes that emphasized comfort and gentle control. But it soon became clear that she was really quite picky. After all, Sara said she knew exactly what she wanted the garment to do—and not do. For example, the bottom edge needed to be snug and secure enough not to roll up, but not so snug that it created discomfort or bulges on either side. She also had specific ideas for the fabric in the crotch and how it should be constructed since her product was meant to replace regular underwear.

As Sara discovered what worked and what didn't, she rejected several early attempts. And because her small project still was not considered an urgent priority by the mill, she often had to wait for them to make her modifications to the design, and then fit in another run on the machines. As a result, the prototype creation process took nearly eight months.

## Tying Up All the Loose Ends

After working a year on the patent and prototype, Sara finally began to let her friends and family in on her little secret. As she'd expected, not everyone understood the idea. Many asked her to explain it and convince them it would work. But by now, she had spent months of work on the project. She had developed expertise in several areas, so their comments didn't discourage her. Soon, almost everyone she told ended up getting behind her and cheering her on.

Time continued to pass. Sara still got up every morning and worked all day at Danka, then worked on her invention at night. In the midst of learning about hosiery and transforming her own paper-clipped designs into a satisfactory prototype, she was also still working on her patent application. Finally, she began wrapping up everything she would be able to do herself. Before she could go back to an attorney to get a quote for the finishing touches, she needed two things: a name for the product and a picture for the application.

Sara had spent much of her free time for months trying to think of the perfect name. "I had spent about a year and a half coming up with really bad names," she said.[32] For a while, her top name idea was really horrifying: "Open-Toed Delilahs." It's hard to imagine that name at the heart of a thriving billion-dollar business. Fortunately, it didn't stick, and Sara continued brainstorming. She began to focus on her observations about two things: sales and comedy. "I knew at the time that Kodak and Coca-Cola were the two most recognized names in the world, so I started playing with them,"[33] she said. What did they have in common that made them work? She concluded that the strong *k* sound in each name seemed to make them easy to remember. Then she thought of a "weird trade secret" she'd learned from some stand-up comedian friends: the *k* sound also tends to make people laugh.[34]

One day, Sara was sitting in her car in Atlanta traffic, using the time to think and play with name possibilities that included the *k* sound. And in one moment, while stopped at a red light, the name *Spanks* came to her mind. She later said she could almost see it written across her dashboard. Pulling over immediately, she wrote the name on a scrap of paper. "I knew it was right immediately," she said.[35] She was so confident that she decided to register and trademark the name that very evening. In her mind, she was still spelling it *Spanks*. But at the last minute, while filling out the form online, she modified it. "I changed the 'ks' to an 'x'," she said, "because I thought it would be more memorable, and easier to trademark."[36] It was, and the name stuck.

Irreverent and a little naughty, the name *Spanx* fit Sara's sense of humor to a T. Now she needed a picture that also fit her aesthetic. By now her artistic mother knew about the idea and was an avid supporter. So, the two of them got together to create the picture. "She stood in our living room and drew the outline of my body, wearing the product," Sara said. The simple cartoonish image portrayed exactly the kind of feeling that Sara wanted her invention to give.

After almost a year of learning patent law and writing the application herself, Sara was finally getting close. "I went back to the one lawyer who gave me a little bit more time of day than the other ones," she said. She explained to him that she had done all of the work on the patent except the claims portion. Then she pleaded with him to write just that section for a discounted price. When he saw all that she'd done on her own, he was blown away. He told her, "You've written basically the entire patent!"[37] Then he offered to complete it over the weekend for a total of $750. This was a price that Sara could stomach, and she agreed. By the following Monday, her application had been submitted.

## Ready for Prime Time

Finally, in the summer of 2000, Sara was in possession of both a patent and a prototype—for Spanx Footless Body-Shaping Pantyhose. In many ways, everything leading up to this had been the hard part. After all, she'd taught herself patent law and learned everything possible about the manufacturing processes and machinery for hosiery products. She had put in the countless hours of work researching and writing the patent application. She had perfected the design of a revolutionary garment. And she had done almost all of this work by herself, on the cheap, while still keeping her day job.

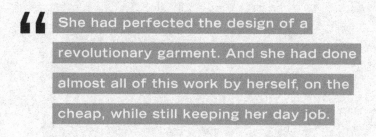

> She had perfected the design of a revolutionary garment. And she had done almost all of this work by herself, on the cheap, while still keeping her day job.

Sara had thought big: she had an idea that she was 100 percent passionate about. She had started small: with her own $5,000, and no outside investors and no debt, she had obtained a patent and created a prototype that would make women both confident and comfortable. This next step of selling was right in her sweet spot. All she had to do was convince women what she believed with 100 percent confidence: Spanx would change their lives. What could possibly go wrong?

## ■ LESSON WE CAN LEARN FROM THE SPANX STORY: DON'T QUIT YOUR DAY JOB

Are you willing to think big and start small? Sara spent two years of her life and all of her savings just doing the groundwork needed to launch Spanx. She worked nights and weekends. To achieve success, don't quit your day job. Take on another job, and work to try to make it your *dream* job.

"If everyone has to think outside the box, maybe it is the box that needs fixing."

—MALCOLM GLADWELL

CHAPTER FOUR

# RESHAPING
# A CATEGORY

I n 2000, with patent and prototype in hand, Sara was ready to
bring Spanx to market, but to understand what she was up
against you'd benefit from a little history about women's undergarments. At the turn of the twenty-first century, shapewear was
out of fashion. True, most women could remember going shopping in the lingerie department with their grandmothers as
young children. Back then, the girdle section filled a sizable
display space, and mature women had several styles and brands
to choose from. But within decades, the shapewear category
would almost completely vanish. Young women had started re-
jecting girdles starting in the 1960s, with the growth of femi-
nism and a "let it all hang out" movement. By the '80s, only
older women wore anything resembling a girdle. And by 1998,
the only shapewear that most women were familiar with was
"granny panties." Not exactly a positive name or association.

· · ·

## An Instrument of Oppression

Of course, girdles were only the most recent trend in women's shapewear. Women had been manipulating their bodies to conform to beauty standards for generations. Before the early 1900s, those in the Western world had endured nearly four hundred years of the most controversial shapewear garment ever: the corset. This stiff and uncomfortable "cage" constricted and squeezed women's torsos, making their waists extremely narrow to fit the clothing styles of the day. Depending on how tightly a woman laced hers up, a corset could keep her from moving freely, make her more likely to faint from lack of oxygen, or even force her internal organs into new locations in her abdomen. Yet, from the late Renaissance to the early twentieth century, some type of corset was considered an essential part of a woman's daily wardrobe. Virtually no respectable woman left her home without one on under her dress.

Eventually, around the 1920s, when women in the United States won the right to vote along with other legal rights, the corset started to fall out of favor. Seen as a symbol of women's oppression by men, the waist-trimming garment was cast off by young women. However, the attempt to mold their own bodies didn't exactly go away; it just migrated. As more form-fitting skirts and trousers were introduced, the girdle—essentially a large pair of underpants constructed of thick, tight elastic—came into being. And women spent the next two generations struggling every day to get into and out of what was essentially a tourniquet for the lower half of the body.

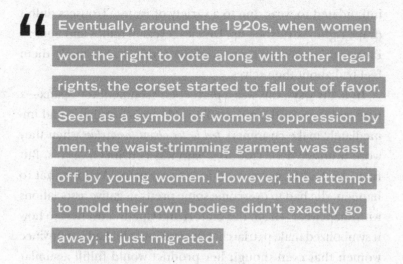

> Eventually, around the 1920s, when women won the right to vote along with other legal rights, the corset started to fall out of favor. Seen as a symbol of women's oppression by men, the waist-trimming garment was cast off by young women. However, the attempt to mold their own bodies didn't exactly go away; it just migrated.

## Internal Girdles and Airbrushed Thighs

Womankind universally hated girdles, even while they still felt compelled to wear them. When the garments finally fell out of fashion, few people were sad to see them go. But ironically, even when girdles disappeared, the pressure on women to conform to unrealistic beauty standards did not.

The "ideal" size actually continued to shrink, with the popularity of smaller and smaller fashion models and Hollywood stars. There was the 1990s popularity of a look known as "heroin chic"; virtually no one besides a 5'10" model who consumed only cigarettes and salad could live up to the standard. Eating disorders exploded, airbrushing became a standard practice in magazines, and studies showed that a majority of American women felt bad about their bodies.

But clothing just kept getting more form-fitting and less forgiving. More and more women found themselves staring into closets feeling mocked by garments they'd bought but were too intimidated to wear due to a variety of issues. Trousers didn't drape right. Skirts rode up. Dresses revealed lumps and bumps. Rather than making them confident, the clothes made them feel bad about themselves.

In many ways, this was a perfect environment for Spanx—a new and improved comfortable undergarment that could immediately make customers *feel better about themselves* when they wore it under their clothing. Sara was convinced of this. But first, she had to get women to try on Spanx. And for that to happen, she had to overcome some pretty negative associations with shapewear—from discomfort and unattractiveness to how it symbolized male patriarchal oppression. She had to convince women that even though her product would fulfill a similar function to old shapewear, it would be completely different.

> ❝ In many ways, this was a perfect environment for Spanx.

## Welcome to Shapewear—the First Rule of Shapewear Is: You Do Not Talk about Shapewear!

Not only did Sara need to overcome women's beliefs about shapewear—she had to start by convincing them to have a conversation about it. Even at this point in the late twentieth century, it was still considered impolite to discuss undergarments in many environments. Sure, Madonna had been wearing them *outside* her clothes for years, and teen fashion included low-rise jeans that exposed underwear—among other things. But, by and large, for adult women in professional settings, a

visible bra strap was still a no-no, and talking about underpants—at least in mixed company—just wasn't done. To illus-
trate how far things have come since then, the vast majority of
adult women in 2000 could still remember watching TV as
children and seeing bra commercials where the garment was
demonstrated on a mannequin torso instead of a real woman.
Why? Because none of the networks allowed TV advertisers to
show actual models in their underwear. This ban remained in
place until 1987.[1]

Fortunately, standards of acceptability were now changing at
lightning speed. As it became harder to shock people, marketing was getting edgier and more humorous. And this was right
in Sara's wheelhouse. Her version of shapewear would not be
so deadly serious. Unlike the "Fight Club" in the movie of that
title, it needed to be talked about. With Spanx as the name, her
product was still pushing the boundaries of the era. After all,
she'd already encountered negative responses from some of
the more conservative hosiery mill owners, so she knew she was
on the edge. But she loved the humor of the name, including
the slightly naughty connotation. Based on her sales experiences, along with a brief foray into stand-up comedy years before, humor had worked in the past as a way to get a foot in the
door. So why not run with it now?

First, she needed a witty slogan. Right away, she actually
came up with two: "Not your grandma's girdle," and "Don't
worry, we've got your butt covered." Besides being funny, they
were relatable. The phrases were things that girlfriends would
find funny in casual conversation. Many women still smiled or
even giggled when hearing the word "butt" in public. The
Spanx name plus the slogans could be like racy remarks at a
bridal shower: making women laugh with a mixture of embarrassment and glee.

## Not Your Grandma's Girdle

Sara made it clear that she wanted her customer to smile at the thought of buying Spanx for herself, rather than dreading it and hoping no one saw her make the purchase. The words she chose for marketing were just her first step in communicating how different her product was from old-fashioned shapewear. She said that *everything* about Spanx needed to be different for women to be convinced. This started with how it looked on the shelf. Rather than blending in with all the products in its department, Spanx needed to stand out. Fortunately, this wouldn't be too difficult because at some point in the modern United States, the lingerie and hosiery departments had turned the exact same shade of beige, gray, or white. To make her package shout, "I'm new, I'm different, check me out,"[2] all that Sara had to do was pick any color other than neutral. She made her flat square Spanx package shiny and bright red. Sara saw the package as revolutionary, later saying she believed that "no one had ever done that in the hosiery space."[3]

The package needed to stand out in other ways as well. Sara wanted the cover design to look cute and young, not stodgy or conservative. Right away, she declared that it would not contain a boring photo of "the same half-naked woman that had been on every package for the last forty years."[4] Instead, she asked a friend with a graphic design degree to help her create a fun image for the cover. Working evenings in the friend's apartment, they made the logo and tagline splashy and exciting. Then, keeping in mind the sleek female silhouette that Sara's mother had sketched for the patent application, they created a similar cartoonish image with a long blonde ponytail, and posed her looking back over her shoulder, wearing a pair of Spanx. Declaring the character Sara's animated alter ego, they named her Sunny.[5]

Soon after, Sara and her friend started work on the back of the package. First, they created a size chart for the back. That part was easy because they had tried different sizes on actual women. Next, the package needed some legalese and instructions, but they had no idea how it should be worded. Once again, because consulting an attorney would cost money, Sara followed her normal pattern. She said she decided to figure it out herself: "I went to the department store and bought ten different pairs of pantyhose." She took them all back to her apartment and laid them out on the floor.[6] Then, studying what was written on the back of each one, she concluded that every sentence that appeared on the majority of the labels needed to be on hers. They wrote and formatted everything, then printed some samples on regular printer paper. When the time came, the packages would be ready to go to print.

## From One Girlfriend to Another, Starting at the Top

With the packaging figured out, Sara was ready to get Spanx in front of customers. Today, someone in her position might try to get on *Shark Tank*, but that TV show wouldn't be around until a few years in the future. Sara wasn't aware of the usual process of convincing stores to carry a new product, so, she did what she knew how to do. She placed a cold call to a high-end department store. Literally, she pulled out the Atlanta phone book and called her local Neiman Marcus.[7]

This was absurd for a few reasons. She called one location of a national chain. Then she gave her pitch to the first person she talked to. This low-level employee probably put Sara on hold and laughed about it with the other salesclerks, then transferred her around until she finally reached the manager. After Sara made her pitch again, the manager must have chuckled before telling Sara that the decision to carry a product wasn't made by an individual store. Instead, the national buyer—who worked at the corporate headquarters in Dallas, Texas—was the person to pitch. Apparently unfazed by any of this, Sara simply asked for and got that phone number. She hung up and immediately placed her next call to Dallas.

This was still not "how things were done" at that time, however. Traditionally, the primary way new manufacturers exposed their products to buyers was at trade shows. They would create a display, rent a booth on the main sales floor at the show, and explain their product to buyers as they walked by. Then they just waited, hoping that a buyer would express interest. This was no instant process. "Getting noticed at trade shows is a route that usually takes years," said author and financial adviser Wes Moss in his book *Starting from Scratch*. If Sara had known about trade shows, he added, "she might have set up her table next to fifty other hopefuls and been overlooked."[8]

Sitting at a booth waiting for customers to stumble upon her product was not Sara's style, anyway. She'd endured the trial by fire of cold-calling and earning her entire income on commission when selling fax machines. The idea of cold-calling the Neiman Marcus buyer in Dallas would not have felt frightening.

## Your Customers Need This Product

As the phone rang on the call to Dallas, Sara's first hurdle was her product name. Spanx seemed to have a polarizing effect—people either loved it or hated it. "I used to hold my breath every time I said it out loud," she said. Many people were "so offended they'd hang up on me."[9] But all Sara could do was forge ahead and hope the buyer would be willing to talk. When the receptionist at Neiman Marcus headquarters answered, Sara plunged right in and asked to speak to the hosiery buyer.

"One moment and I'll connect you."

She'd made it past the first gatekeeper! Sara waited with her pitch as the phone rang and rang, but it went to voice mail. She left a short, clear, cheerful message with her big pitch: her product would change the way women wore clothes.[10] After leaving her contact information, she hung up. When she didn't hear from the buyer that day or the next, she called again, and left a message again. The next day, she called at a different time of day, hoping the buyer would be available to pick up the phone. Again, a message. "I called for days at different times," she said later.

Finally, the buyer returned her call. Immediately using her best sales techniques, Sara worked to find a connection with the woman on the other end of the line. She briefly explained her invention, and how it could help Neiman Marcus's customers. The buyer listened politely, but she didn't seem enthusiastic. So Sara played the only other card she could think of: she offered to fly from Atlanta to Dallas, if the buyer would give her just ten minutes to pitch the invention in person. Something about that made the buyer say yes. And Sara bought a ticket and got on a plane right away.

## Prepared for the Meeting in the Boardroom

On the hot summer day when Sara arrived in Dallas, she drove from the airport to the elegant building housing the Neiman

Marcus headquarters. In the clothes she'd chosen for the meeting—which featured the original white slacks and sandals—she appeared professional and polished. But on her shoulder was something her friends had begged her not to bring: her well-worn red Eastpak backpack that she'd used all through college. They had urged her to buy an expensive bag just for this meeting, to make the best possible impression. Instead, she proclaimed the red backpack her "good luck charm."[11] Now she carried it on her back, containing her prototype in a Ziploc storage bag along with a color photocopy of her packaging.

After greetings were exchanged with the buyer and some other executives, Sara set her unique red "briefcase" on the table and dove into her pitch. Calling on all of her sales experience and enthusiasm, Sara told her own story of how she had searched in 1998 for a product that didn't exist: something that would allow her to look great and feel confident in snug pants and sandals.

She shared how her own experience had convinced her that a huge need existed for this product, so she had invented Spanx Footless Body-Shaping Pantyhose to meet it. She insisted her invention would change women's lives and how they wore clothes. And, passing her prototype around to the corporate executives, she assured them that even in a tough hosiery market, Spanx would sell. Why? Because they were the only pantyhose made for women, by a woman. She told them Spanx would make a woman feel not only confident, but comfortable in her clothing. Her product was a garment that would make women feel good *about themselves.*

But the allotted ten minutes were flying by, and Sara was losing her audience. And possibly her only shot. She has described what happened many times over the years since then.

"I suggested she come with me to the bathroom. To be honest, she was a bit taken aback."[12] Sara explained that if she could just *show* the buyer what she meant, with an actual "before and after" demonstration, the product would make a lot more sense. Amazingly, the buyer agreed, and the two women walked to the closest restroom.

## And for the Real Meeting in the Restroom

Sara entered, followed by the buyer. But as the door was still closing behind them, Sara suddenly stopped in her tracks and blurted, "Take a look at my butt!" She gestured at her own rear end in the soon-to-be-famous white pants. (She later said she had intentionally worn regular underpants rather than Spanx under them.) After shamelessly pointing out her own cellulite and panty lines, Sara asked the buyer to wait, then disappeared into the nearest stall. Sara did a quick change, threw open the door, and emerged in the same outfit—but this time with her Spanx prototype under the pants. She whirled around, turning her back to the buyer, and gestured to her bottom again.

"See what I mean?"

The buyer obediently looked again at her backside. Of course, Sara was wearing the same pants, but they now draped beautifully on her lineless, smooth, firm lower half.

Then the buyer said the words that would change everything: "I get it. It's brilliant!"[13]

Sara was right. That one look was all it took.

■ **LESSON WE CAN LEARN FROM THE SPANX STORY: LEARN HOW TO SELL**

No matter what career path you're following, salesmanship is a skill worth cultivating. About this, Sara said, "Cold-call selling teaches you the most unbelievable life skills. It teaches you how to get your foot in the door or win somebody over in 30 seconds or less. It teaches you perseverance and to keep going, especially when people aren't necessarily kind or friendly to you." Sara also credited her experience in cold calling, along with her participation in debate in school, with teaching her to "see both sides of an issue and also to speak quickly on your feet and articulate yourself clearly."[14]

At this point, things for Spanx began moving very quickly. After returning to the conference room, the buyer made an incredible offer: to order five thousand units to test in seven Neiman Marcus stores in various parts of the country. If they sold well, she said, the chain would consider ordering more.[15] Sara somehow managed to accept the offer, thank the buyer, make the necessary arrangements, and say her goodbyes.

## Is This Really Happening?

Soon, Sara was on the phone, dialing a familiar number in North Carolina. After Sam Kaplan picked up, she exclaimed, "Sam! Sam, it's Sara! I need more. I just landed Neiman Marcus." Years later in an interview for NPR, she recounted the exchange:

"He paused. There was nothing on the other end of the phone for what seemed like a minute."

She asked if he was still there. "Sara, don't take this the wrong way," he responded, "but I thought you were going to give these away as Christmas gifts or something." Then, after another pause: "What do you *mean*, Neiman Marcus just took it?"[16]

And just like that, Spanx was in business. Sam might have needed some time to get over his shock, but he started production on the garments as soon as possible. Soon, the first five thousand pairs of Spanx Footless Body-Shaping Pantyhose were on the assembly line. Two weeks later, the first order departed the plant for the seven Neiman Marcus test stores.

Many inventors would have paused to celebrate after finding a buyer for their product and fulfilling a big order. Especially for a high-end retailer like Neiman Marcus. They might even sit back and think, "I've hit the big time!" But that wasn't Sara's response. In fact, she later said, "That is the biggest mistake that entrepreneurs make."[17] After landing Neiman Marcus would come the *real* work—convincing individual shoppers to purchase her product. It was her time to shine.

## Applause Is Contagious

Just three weeks after Sara's trip to Dallas, her products appeared on the racks in the test stores. Even before that, she had already called several family members, close friends, casual acquaintances, and even people she hadn't talked to in years. If someone she knew lived within driving distance of a Neiman Marcus store that was selling her product, she probably called them.

On each call, Sara explained her invention to the person. Then she asked for a big favor: Would they be willing to go into their store and ask sales staff about Spanx Footless Body-Shaping Pantyhose? Then make a big deal of how excited they were about it? And then buy a pair? If they would do all of these things, she would mail them a check for $20, the retail price.[18] Offering to reimburse dozens of people from her own limited funds might not seem to be a wise decision, but it was a great strategy to build interest and sales in all seven stores. It had the added advantage of attracting the interest of each store's sales staff. If they liked it, they might embrace the product's value and share it with their loyal customers. And Sara's strategy worked. As her friends came through and begged for Spanx, word of product interest and sales numbers began to reach Neiman Marcus headquarters.

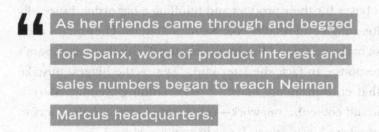

> **As her friends came through and begged for Spanx, word of product interest and sales numbers began to reach Neiman Marcus headquarters.**

## But Don't Take My Word for It! Look at This Gigantic Picture of My Butt!

At this point, Sara had successfully recruited others to build enthusiasm and buzz for Spanx. But with her proven ability to sell, it's no surprise that her next strategy relied on her *own* ability to get people excited. She would not leave sales of Spanx up to other people if there was a way for her to personally influence customers.

Since Neiman Marcus had chosen her hometown of Atlanta as one of the test cities, as soon as they were on the local store's shelves, she asked if she could set up a table there to talk to shoppers in person. They said yes, so she went right away to an office store and ordered blown-up prints of two photos of her rear end: one wearing the white pants and ordinary undergarments, and one from the same angle in the same pants but wearing Spanx underneath. Then, she showed up at the Atlanta Neiman Marcus for the first of several evenings. Setting up her table in the hosiery area, she laid out her cheerful red packages of Spanx and watched for approaching shoppers.

Standing beside her table display, holding up before-and-after photos of her own rear end, Sara struck up a conversation with every woman who walked by. She then explained how Spanx would change their lives and expand their wardrobes and showed them the two photos of her backside. First the one without Spanx, showing off life-size cellulite. Then she showed them the one with Spanx, pointing out how panty lines and cellulite had disappeared. The same pants clearly appeared looser and draped better on her physique, which was suddenly firmer and smaller. Her use of her own rear view had to be strategic, because it was essentially saying, "We're in this together," and "let me share this with you and tell you why it's in my wardrobe." That personal connection and the camaraderie of women would make all the difference.[19]

## A Mission Worth Crying Over

Women responded positively to her pitch, and Sara expanded her one-woman show to the other test stores. But because they were spread around the United States, she would have to travel to do so. That was a problem. True, she had already done a fair amount of traveling with Danka, but it wasn't something she enjoyed. In fact, she especially hated it if any leg of the trip was on an airplane.

For as long as she could remember, Sara had suffered from an intense fear of heights and flying. It wasn't strong enough to completely keep her from getting on a plane, but she tended to avoid it unless she had a really compelling reason. Spanx certainly fit that bill, so she scheduled a few trips for her days off. And thus, Sara found herself in the air several times in a short period of time. According to her reminiscences in dozens of interviews over decades, in every instance, her seatmates always witnessed exactly what flying did to her. To this day, she still hates it. This is how she described the experience as recently as 2015: "I am so stressed every time I take off, I basically have a panic attack."[20] Sara would eventually come up with a strategy to cope as well as she could: it involved a bag of Cheez-Its (her favorite snack), noise-canceling headphones, and a favorite song. Still, tears and panic would travel with her for years to come. Her decision in 2000 to travel by air to sell Spanx could not have been made lightly.

## Buzz Builder

In every store, Sara shared her infectious enthusiasm about her invention. Some women lingered and listened and picked up a package. Sara's personal story—and the visible proof they saw on her rear end—offered hope. And one by one, they began to buy.

When Sara's brand-new Spanx customers went home and tried the product on under their own clothes, it probably became clear that she was not exaggerating. And then something amazing began to happen: when these Spanx wearers received compliments, whether from friends or complete strangers, some of them replied with more than a polite "thank you." They also didn't pretend that they worked out constantly or were just "born this way." And they didn't give in to embarrassment and avoid mentioning shapewear. Instead, these customers became avid evangelists for the product, even showing their undergarments to total strangers. The good feelings and excitement of more and more brand evangelists spilled out as they told everyone their "secret": Spanx.

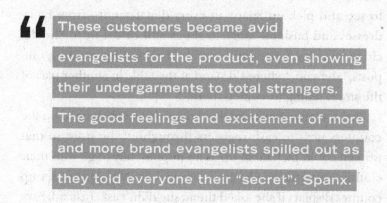

**These customers became avid evangelists for the product, even showing their undergarments to total strangers. The good feelings and excitement of more and more brand evangelists spilled out as they told everyone their "secret": Spanx.**

Sara even encountered enthusiastic customers who came back to share their success stories with her. New shoppers would sometimes spot her display from across the store, march purposefully up to the table, and pick up a package in their size with no prompting from her. When she said hello and told them she was the inventor, their faces lit up. But before she could tell them anything about Spanx, they started telling *her* all about what the product could do, based on what they'd witnessed on a friend's backside. And the number of women who went to a Neiman Marcus to shop for Spanx steadily increased.

## Pushing the Envelope

This was all fantastic news. Just a few days into the Neiman Marcus test run, Spanx were flying off shelves at the test stores. But Sara was still churning out other ideas. One day in her local store, she decided that she really wasn't satisfied with the one place where Spanx were displayed—in the hosiery section. "I realized that my product was in the sleepiest part of the department store. It was back in the corner and nobody was going there,"[21] she explained. In her mind, women ought to be able to see and pick up Spanx in every department—from fancy dresses and business attire to shoes and casual wear. She decided to move her table around. "I ended up creating outposts," she said, "where I'd stand at the table in another part of the store, selling to women there."[22]

Sara was also convinced that Spanx displays belonged on the counters next to cash registers throughout the store so that women could pick them up as an impulse buy to go with their clothing purchases. Since no one was likely to let her set up counter displays if she asked them, she didn't ask. Instead, Sara once again worked on her own to make something happen. She made a trip to Target, where she bought several vertical desktop stands designed to hold envelopes. She loaded each one with packages of Spanx. The next day, back at the Atlanta Neiman Marcus, she stealthily placed one big red Spanx display on the counter in front of every cash register in the store. Employees saw them, but they thought this new Spanx promotion had been approved by someone else in the company. As a result, the unsanctioned displays stayed in place for a while— until Sara took her efforts just a little too far. One evening, when one stand kept falling over, she affixed it to the counter with packing tape. When she arrived at the store the next evening, a sales associate approached her and said, "We need to talk. They have you on surveillance camera."[23]

Sara's DIY tactics had come to light. But they had *also* increased her sales as she'd hoped. Even if she shouldn't have done it without approval, the initiative had been successful. And when the company leadership was told, they ended up saying, "Whatever this girl's doing, let her keep doing it."[24]

She did. And only two weeks after the initial order of five thousand was put on display in the seven test stores, Sara received another call from the Neiman Marcus buyer. "You're never going to believe this," said the buyer. "We've sold out of the product."[25] Every single pair of Spanx had sold out at every test store. The Neiman Marcus buyer was now calling to place a much larger order for all thirty-two of their stores. The machinery in Sam's mill started working immediately.

During the same two weeks Sara had spent flying all over the country to hawk Spanx in the test stores, she was also in conversations with additional department store chains. Those chains had declined to order initially because they wanted to see what would happen with the Neiman Marcus test. When Neiman Marcus ordered more, two of those other chains took action and placed their own sizable orders. Soon, bright red Spanx packages could also be found in the hosiery departments of Saks Fifth Avenue and Bloomingdale's.

## From Impossible Dream to Amazing Reality

In the course of two years, Sara had turned what we'd call a "side hustle" into the job she had dreamed about. "I didn't want to quit my job," Sara explained. "I needed the income and the security and the insurance and the health benefits and all that."[26] So she'd kept working full-time at Danka while working more than full-time on Spanx. She trained salespeople for office machinery every weekday, and then spent every night and every weekend on Spanx. Even after she got her product into Neiman Marcus, she just spent every evening at a store until closing, then strategized late into the night. She had already pushed herself to the limit. While she was at Danka all day, Sara said, "the semi-trucks would drop boxes of Spanx outside my apartment."[27] Every shipment of product from North Carolina arrived at her tiny apartment. Every night, she packed orders in her living room. Every morning on her way to work, she dropped them off at Mail Boxes Etc. to be shipped out. With the newer, larger orders placed by Neiman Marcus, Saks, and Bloomingdale's, things would only get busier. Shipments were getting larger.

Sara finally had the proof she needed that her product would make it. Spanx was generating revenue and sales were growing. The time for a decision had arrived. Logistically, it made the most sense for her to be available at her home "headquarters" whenever a shipment arrived. "That was when I got the courage to make the leap and go on my own," she said.[28] On October 14, 2000, Sara Blakely quit her job at Danka.

## What the . . . ?

On a sunny afternoon two weeks later, at the end of October, Sara's phone rang. Answering, she heard an unfamiliar voice. This person said she was calling from Chicago. "I'm with Oprah Winfrey's production company," she continued. "We'd like to feature you and your product on Oprah's show two weeks from now. When can we travel to Atlanta to film?"

## ■ LESSON WE CAN LEARN FROM THE SPANX STORY: MAKE YOUR OWN LUCK

Sara did everything in her power to make Spanx successful, from taking embarrassing photographs of herself to demonstrate the product, to working in stores for free on nights and weekends, to jumping on planes at her own expense, to reimbursing people who would buy her product to get the word out. In what area of your life are you waiting for opportunity instead of going out and working for it? There's a reason people call it a "side hustle." Because it takes hustle!

"You get in life what you have the courage to ask for."

—OPRAH WINFREY

CHAPTER FIVE

# MAKING SPANX A HOUSEHOLD NAME

**F**or most ordinary small business owners, a call from Oprah Winfrey's Harpo Studios would come as a total shock. Sara was certainly caught by surprise when it happened, but she would later explain that it wasn't completely out of the blue. She listened as the Harpo employee explained that Oprah herself had chosen her and her product, Spanx, to appear alongside dozens of others on that year's "Oprah's Favorite Things" episode. Sara and Spanx would appear on TV in millions of households on November 17, 2000. The caller wondered if perhaps Sara had heard of "Oprah's Favorite Things"?

## Her Favorite Things

*Of course*, Sara knew about it. Oprah Winfrey's annual pre-Christmas episode, also known as her "Favorite Things" show, was the hottest studio audience ticket in television. Because it had a reputation as a massive giveaway-fest, the taping date was shrouded in secrecy, and tickets were extremely hard to come by. Audience members always whooped and jumped for joy when they found out they had arrived for *that* taping. Then, throughout the entire episode, the screaming continued. Everyone knew that after Oprah named and described each "favorite thing" choice, everyone in the studio audience would receive one. Even for those who only saw it on TV, this was one of Oprah's most anticipated episodes every year. For the holiday season, everyone wanted to give and/or receive the gifts that Oprah had recommended.

According to Jack Neff, writing for *Ad Age* in 2008, Oprah Winfrey was "the very pinnacle of product publicity."[1] Her TV show, on the air nationwide from 1986 to 2011, was consistently the top-rated daytime show in the United States. And in 2000, it was at the height of its popularity, averaging seven million viewers per episode.[2] The audience for the "Oprah's Favorite Things" episode always exceeded that average. And behind every "favorite thing" was a manufacturer that knew they had hit the big time. Products that were endorsed by Oprah were almost guaranteed a massive sales spike through a phenomenon that became known as the Oprah Effect.

In the minutes and hours and days after any product appeared on Oprah's show, companies saw their orders increase exponentially. Many became multimillion-dollar businesses overnight. But some businesses—the smaller ones in particular—found it challenging to keep up. The entire experience—from rushing to prepare a lot more product and filling thousands of orders, to fixing crashed websites and working nearly twenty-four hours a day—often threw their businesses into turmoil in the months that followed. But afterward, the vast majority said that if they had the opportunity, they'd do it all again.

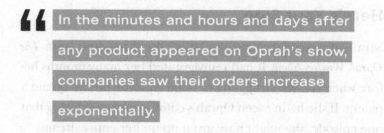

**" In the minutes and hours and days after any product appeared on Oprah's show, companies saw their orders increase exponentially.**

## The Power of Oprah

Analysts believe that Oprah's endorsement had such great power due to her personal style and authenticity. She was very strategic and particular about what she gave her official "blessing" to. It was always something she personally liked and usually used. Analyst Clay Halton, writing in Investopedia, said, "Oprah chose products she was genuinely interested in, rather than being paid to promote them."[3] Hers was the ultimate word-of-mouth recommendation, from her mouth to millions of ears.

For Oprah's mostly female audience, she was also their friend and confidante, the woman they invited into their living rooms every afternoon. Oprah was consistently honest and open, which made her relatable. Everyone knew about her past experiences, dreams, and struggles. And when Oprah said something would change your life, you believed her. She was just the kind of girlfriend an inventor would want in her corner, which meant Sara had done more than wait and hope for her call.

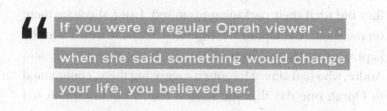

**" If you were a regular Oprah viewer . . . when she said something would change your life, you believed her.**

## Here's Your Sign

Sara had never forgotten the "sign" she'd received from *The Oprah Winfrey Show*. It had reinvigorated her many months before when she was struggling to build a prototype and obtain a patent. If she hadn't seen Oprah's cutoff pantyhose during that one episode, she might have given up on her entire dream.

Sara remained grateful, so when the first order of Spanx arrived at her apartment that past summer, she created a gift basket for Oprah Winfrey. Filling it with several pairs of Spanx, she included a handwritten personal note of thanks to Oprah for that influential episode. And then, showing typical chutzpah, Sara concluded the note with, "I want you to have this, and I want to get on your show."[4]

After boxing everything up, Sara addressed the package to Oprah's longtime stylist Andre Walker, and dropped it in the mail. And after that, she didn't spend a lot of time thinking about it. She was still too busy back then, working her full-time job along with rearranging Neiman Marcus stores and convincing friends to buy Spanx on her behalf. But the package, containing the note and the basket of Spanx Footless Body-Shaping Pantyhose, actually arrived on Walker's desk, most likely piled with hundreds of gifts from other savvy entrepreneurs. But for some reason, Walker took a look at Sara's box. And in a decision that would change the course of Sara's life, he included her product to be worn under some of Oprah's wardrobe for the show. He even encouraged Oprah to give them a try, to see if they did what their packaging promised. Later, she wore them on the show. And Oprah Winfrey liked Spanx so much that she kept wearing them—even off the air. Some time passed, and Andre, who had almost forgotten suggesting them, commented to Oprah one day that she looked like she'd lost about ten pounds. Flattered, she replied that she hadn't lost weight. But she *was* wearing those Spanx he'd recommended, and she loved how they made her feel. After that, Spanx became a regular part of Oprah's wardrobe. So, when it came time to choose her favorite things, adding Spanx to the list was obvious.

## A Perfect Pair

Oprah Winfrey was really the ideal person to endorse Spanx, and not just because of her power and influence as OPRAH. Always open about her struggles as well as her victories, Oprah had shared one struggle very honestly with her audience over the years: her ongoing battle with weight and physical health.

When Oprah put on a slimming and smoothing pair of Spanx, they did for her exactly what they'd done for Sara: they gave her a more positive attitude about her own body. She felt more physically comfortable and emotionally confident in Spanx than she had in any other pantyhose or shapewear.

The samples from Sara might have felt to Oprah like they were invented just for her. In a way, they kind of were, since not long after Oprah had shown her entire viewing audience her problem with pantyhose and sandals, a member of that audience, Sara, had created the perfect solution and sent it to her. It could easily be argued that Spanx were perfect for Oprah, and Oprah was perfect for Spanx.

## A Polaroid Picture

After Sara agreed to a date for Oprah's people to film in Atlanta, she hung up the phone. With that phone call, a fuzzy picture that she had imagined for nearly a decade began to come into sharper focus. It was a picture Oprah's producer could not have known about.

Years before, while Sara was still in high school and memorizing her dad's Wayne Dyer tapes, she took particular note of one thing Dyer advised: the visualization of goals. He taught that when people create "mental snapshots" of the specific future they want to have, they become more likely to attain it. Years passed. Then, when Sara was around twenty years old, she took a very specific "Polaroid picture," as she later called it.[5] In this mental snapshot, she was on *The Oprah Winfrey Show*, being interviewed personally by Oprah. But it wasn't clear in her mind what they were talking about. She also had only a vague idea of what she was wearing, and their surroundings were hazy. But here's what she said was vivid to her: Oprah and herself, seated in chairs across from each other onstage, talking.

Over the next several years, that mental image was a touchpoint for Sara. She often tried to guess what she and Oprah could possibly be talking about in an interview. What could she accomplish that might get her invited onto the show? At first, she assumed getting on Oprah's show would have something to do with her intended law career. Later, when that dream went south and she briefly experimented with stand-up comedy, she wondered if she would achieve fame in *that* career.[6]

After Sara was hired by Danka, there didn't seem to be any way that selling fax machines would bring Oprah-level fame. So, for nearly seven years, the details of her mental image remained a mystery. When she got the call from Oprah's producers, her snapshot finally gained clarity.

The exact picture she'd held onto for nearly a decade would not yet be coming to life, since she wouldn't sit onstage with

Oprah for this particular episode. But she was taking a huge step in that direction. "I was beyond thrilled and excited," she said later. "But I wasn't that surprised."[7]

## How Ready Are You?

Sara soon spoke again with *The Oprah Winfrey Show* producer—this time about logistics. They set a date and time for filming of the background piece in Atlanta. Then came the question the producers asked every supplier of a product that would appear on Oprah: "How ready is your company for the air date? Will you have enough product in stock?"

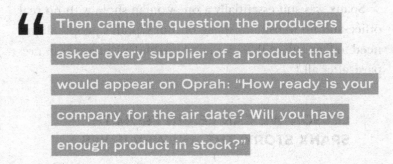

Then came the question the producers asked every supplier of a product that would appear on Oprah: "How ready is your company for the air date? Will you have enough product in stock?"

Oprah's producers had learned from experience to warn companies to get ready for an explosion in sales on the day a show with her endorsement aired. In Sara's case, that was less than three weeks away, but Sara expressed confidence that she would have plenty of inventory at headquarters before the show's air date, ready to ship immediately. Then she was asked, "Will your team be able to handle the workload?"

"Absolutely. We'll be ready."

"How about your website? Orders after the show have crashed other business sites before. Can your servers handle a big increase in traffic?"

Sara assured them that her website was up and ready. Satisfied, they congratulated her again on being chosen and ended the call.

Alone on the couch in her "Spanx headquarters" apartment, Sara might have looked around, wondering where she would stack all the extra packages of products. For her "team," she would call on friends and family members for a day of order-packing on November 18, offering to fuel them with free pizza and wine. Finally, she asked her then-boyfriend to help her build the Spanx website—which didn't yet exist.

"How? I'm a healthcare consultant!" he exclaimed.[8]

Spanx was still essentially a one-woman show, with no real office and no website to speak of. But Oprah's people didn't need to know all of that. Sara had two and a half weeks to prepare, after all.[9]

## LESSON WE CAN LEARN FROM THE SPANX STORY: THE ANSWER IS YES

When Oprah Winfrey's people called, Sara's answer was yes. Yes, I'd love to be on the show. Yes, we'll have enough inventory. Yes, our website will work. She didn't allow what *wasn't yet ready* to stop her from saying yes and getting ready. Do you have that kind of attitude? Say yes, and then figure it out? Say yes, and then work to the deadline? If you want to be successful in business, say yes. Then make it work!

## The Scramble

Sara's first problem to solve was inventory. With the profits from the Neiman Marcus test, the latest retail orders had been placed and were being assembled by Sam's company. They would be shipped directly to the three department stores. That meant the stores would definitely have enough in stock on the day of the show. Sara immediately made another big order to be shipped directly to her apartment before the show date. This inventory would be used to fill any orders Spanx received directly.

With a "staff" of friends and family who agreed to work for food and drink, Spanx would be prepared to package and ship all the direct orders. Now, all they needed was a website where people could place those orders! How hard could that be?

As it turned out, the design and setup of a professional retail website were a little more challenging than imagined. Sara had to poll several friends before she found someone with the expertise to help her. In the end, a very minimalistic site went live, based on a simple color scan of the physical package.[10] It wasn't fancy, but it enabled people to submit and pay for orders. So it would have to do the job for the time being.

But website and product were not the only concerns in the run-up to the Oprah show appearance. Sara had to prepare herself for the upcoming filming of the Spanx feature "package" that was supposed to air during the show.

## The Magic of Television

After Oprah's film crew arrived in Atlanta, they called Sara to run some possible setups and shots by her. They explained that one shot would be of Sara on a sofa, watching the Oprah episode where she cut the feet off her pantyhose. Another would be of Sara pitching the product to the manager of a little boutique—and being told no. But before those setups, they asked to get some footage of Sara and her staff in her headquarters.

When the rental car pulled up in front of Sara's apartment, she was outside waiting to greet the film crew. She presented them with "Spanx headquarters." As they took in her tiny living room, she described it as the closest thing she had to a "staff meeting room."

"Can you pull together your staff for a meeting right now?" they asked.

"Sure! I'll round them up! Give me just a few minutes."

Once again, Sara picked up the phone. She later said she called several local friends, asking them to "quickly leave their jobs and come to my apartment and look like they worked for me." Describing the faux staff meeting for the cameras, she said everyone just sat in a circle on the floor.[11]

The crew also filmed some shots of Sara looking at her backside in a mirror (while wearing the white pants, of course) and just strolling through a mall. She spoke to the camera about how she didn't like the look of her own feet covered in regular pantyhose. And finally, after convincing one of her best friends from childhood to model Spanx Footless Body-Shaping Pantyhose for the cameras, Sara demonstrated and described some of the benefits of her product.

The film crew departed after they'd gotten what they needed, and then all Sara and her loved ones could do was wait until the show's air date.

## The Moment of Truth

Oprah's "Favorite Things" episode for 2000 aired on November 17. Sara and her family and friends in Atlanta saw it on TV. They watched Oprah tell the millions of people in her TV audience that she absolutely loved Spanx and what they did for her shape.

Right away, as Oprah's people had predicted, orders started pouring in. And the flow of orders didn't slow right away. Day after day, Sara and her team of friends and family worked tirelessly to pack, address, and ship order after order. With the push from Oprah, Spanx was profitable from the very beginning. And through the rest of November and all of December, sales kept up a steady growth, both online and in stores. Starting with the original test order from Neiman Marcus, all Spanx sales in 2000 occurred during the final third of the year. By December 31, 2000, Sara's one product, the $20 Footless Body-Shaping Pantyhose, had produced $400,000 in revenue, with a pretax profit margin of 25 percent.[12]

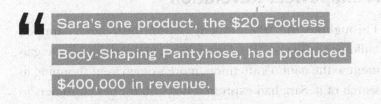

" Sara's one product, the $20 Footless Body-Shaping Pantyhose, had produced $400,000 in revenue.

Sara had run Spanx as a one-woman show since 1998. Even though her dream was massive, she had started and remained small for as long as she could. Because of that, she had avoided common mistakes made by many entrepreneurs. She had no investors to pay and no one but herself to answer to. She had no debt. Overhead was low, with no separate office.

During the first six months of Spanx sales, revenue rose steadily, but so did the need for labor to manage the website, keep up with the finances, and fill orders. It was an exciting, energizing time, but something needed to change. Sara couldn't single-handedly run an exploding business out of a small apartment for much longer. Doing the order fulfillment and shipping by herself became more and more time-consuming and complicated. Friends and family helped when they could, often in exchange for pizza and wine. But it was clearly still too much work for Sara and her small crew.

Near the end of December, Sara was finally busy enough and profitable enough to make some changes. She hired her first two paid staff members: a friend from high school who took care of the books and handled strategy, and another friend who handled marketing. Then she did something to lift a huge load from her shoulders—and her kitchen table. She hired a fulfillment firm to manage inventory and ship orders.[13]

## A Shapewear Revolution

Throughout the 2000 holiday season, buzz never stopped building for Spanx. After Oprah brought this unique undergarment to the nation's attention, more women went shopping in search of it. Sara had expressed her wish for her customers to feel like they were buying a present for themselves. And, lo and behold, it seemed that they *were* buying Spanx for themselves, even during the Christmas gift-giving season. Soon, Footless Body-Shaping Pantyhose were present beneath both fancy and casual attire at holiday parties around the country that December. And many women at those parties felt so good about the effect of Spanx on their bodies that they not only admitted wearing them, they volunteered the information to their female friends. Many pant legs were lifted to flash the bottom edge of their Spanx. In the days and weeks following those parties, more women who had witnessed Spanx in action went shopping for them in the shapewear department.

It was fortunate that the Spanx red package was easy to spot among all the beige, because Sara's product turned out to be challenging for retailers to categorize. Merchandising staff were not certain about where to display them. The product had "pantyhose" in the name, but it smoothed and slimmed like a girdle. However, unlike girdles, it actually felt comfortable—more like control-top pantyhose. Yet, Spanx was an improvement over traditional pantyhose in many ways—aside from the missing feet. Spanx met needs for female wearers that had never been addressed by the old brands. They offered all-over comfort, so women could easily wear them all day. Their wide waist and leg bands were knitted with nylon thread, absent any tight elastic. Thus, they created no dents or bulges on the leg or waistline. The crotch panel was composed of cotton, which allowed women to comfortably wear them alone, without other underpants. And their smoothing effect extended from waist to lower leg, erasing cellulite and sometimes even decreasing a woman's dress size.

At $20 per pair, Spanx Footless Body-Shaping Pantyhose cost quite a bit more than most pantyhose brands. But they were designed to be a durable and reusable undergarment, unlike the fragile and disposable product that ordinary pantyhose had been. So, inspired by hearing Oprah and then their own friends raving about Spanx, many shoppers took the plunge and paid a little more for one pair as an experiment. And often, all it took was wearing that one pair for them to see and feel the benefits and value. In the wake of that, the name Spanx was becoming synonymous with the category, like

Kleenex is to tissue and Google is to search engines. Of course, competitors would soon rush copycats into the market. But when women shopped for something to wear to smooth everything out under a form-fitting dress, they usually said they were going in search of Spanx.

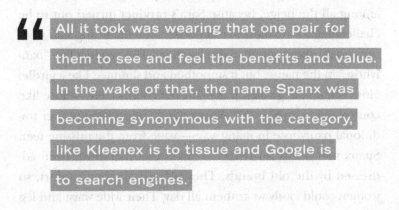

> All it took was wearing that one pair for them to see and feel the benefits and value. In the wake of that, the name Spanx was becoming synonymous with the category, like Kleenex is to tissue and Google is to search engines.

## You're Going to Hollywood

At the same time that Spanx was increasing in sales and popularity among ordinary women, Sara's invention started to attract attention in Hollywood. When Spanx first arrived there, no one who wore them seemed to be showing them off. But word soon got around anyway, from personal stylists to wardrobe departments for TV shows and movies. These fashion experts quietly discussed how great Spanx could make the stars look in the tightest clothing. Movie stars' stylists saw a new miracle tool to make their clients look amazing—and it didn't require a 24/7 workout regimen, or a crash diet, or a visit to a cosmetic surgeon. And, of course, actresses watched Oprah, too. A few requested them from stylists or wardrobe departments. Others shopped for the product directly.

After wearing Footless Body-Shaping Pantyhose under snug trousers and gowns, and realizing how they looked and felt, movie stars continued wearing them. Eventually, even directors became aware of how well Spanx worked, along with how willing actresses were to wear them. The garment became more and more common both at awards shows and on set, sometimes even openly discussed. Only two years later, many in the industry would give Spanx credit for how svelte they looked, but in those early months, Sara's invention was still mostly "Hollywood's Big Secret." Even though this was years before the rise of social media and the professional "influencers" of today, Spanx was getting noticed—and talked about—by people who had substantial influence for the early 2000s.

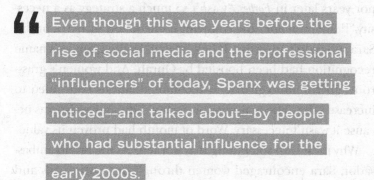

> Even though this was years before the rise of social media and the professional "influencers" of today, Spanx was getting noticed—and talked about—by people who had substantial influence for the early 2000s.

While word got out about Spanx in Hollywood, journalists were also calling to request interviews with Sara, who happily obliged. In fact, she said yes to so many interviews and profiles that she was soon the face and voice of the company to the world. The media loved to tell the rags-to-riches story of a fax machine saleswoman turning into a fashion mogul. Viewers and readers ate it up. People also tended to love Sara, herself. She assured all women that her invention could help them, sharing the story and benefits of Spanx with the media over and over and over again. Soon, the reporters turned around and praised Sara Blakely and Spanx for "reinventing the girdle"—in newspapers and magazines, as well as on the internet, TV, and radio. And sales kept rising.

## Not on the To-Do List

The one thing Spanx did not do in those early months was traditional advertising. Sara said she didn't even consider it at first, because there was no room in her original $5,000 budget. Her choice to rely on word of mouth, said writer Clare O'Connor years later in *Forbes*, "wasn't so much a strategy as a necessity."[14] But even after the company immediately turned a profit, Sara still didn't advertise. It helped that, by then, Spanx's name recognition had been boosted by Oprah. And women's grassroots girlfriend-to-girlfriend recommendations continued to increase sales. The main reason Spanx didn't advertise was because it wasn't necessary. Word of mouth had proven its value.

Why mess with something that worked? As the brand ambassador, Sara encouraged women through her own words and actions to join her as Spanx cheerleaders. She did this by being funny and real. Her silly and "inappropriate" name, slogan, and cartoonish images were chosen out of a belief that they would make people smile. After years of cold-calling to sell fax machines, Sara knew that laughter could buy her twenty more seconds to make her pitch. Fairly immune to rejection or embarrassment, she also wasn't afraid to look silly or foolish. She just stayed true to herself all the time.

Sara's goal of staying real and authentic meant every word used to describe Spanx was intentionally casual and unpretentious. This included even the information on the back of the package. They didn't write about her pantyhose in flowery language. Sara would not use the phrasing that she mockingly quoted as "the sheerest of the sheerest most sheer elegance." Instead, the company came right out and clearly said Spanx "makes your butt look better." Whether in sizing instructions or interview answers, Spanx messaging sounded like a chat with a girlfriend. All of this made Sara and the product relatable. Many women connected so much with her "it's just us girls here—let's be real" attitude that they adopted it as well. They became more and more bold in talking about their shapewear.

Of course, not everyone laughed *with* Spanx, especially at first. In some areas of the country, people refused to laugh because Sara's attitude and the name she'd chosen for her product offended their sensibilities. And some writers and comedians had a field day, making fun of everything about the company, as well as Sara herself. But when people made fun of the product, it meant they were talking about it. Sara said she intentionally welcomed and encouraged the jokes. "By infusing humor wherever I could," she said, "I ended up turning my product into something people love to joke about." Sara believed her strategy seemed to be working, because people kept talking, as she said, "about pantyhose, one of the world's most boring topics."[15]

Spanx might have started out as a small novelty invention. Now it was a huge, popular product, becoming more successful every day. And Sara was no longer a single inventor trying to get people to believe in her. Revenue was flooding in, and she was pouring most of it back into the company. And she continued

"Sustaining a successful business is a hell of a lot of work, and staying hungry is half the battle."

—WENDY TAN WHITE,
Cofounder and CEO of MoonFruit

## CHAPTER SIX

# MAKING SPANX A COMPANY

I t's often said that a lot can change in a year. In Sara's case, a lot had changed in four months. When January 1, 2001, arrived, it was evident from a look back at the final four months of the previous year that a single product launch had transformed Sara from a salaried corporate employee to a self-employed entrepreneur, from a fledgling inventor to a full-fledged business owner, from a someday dreamer to an everyday marketplace doer. Her invention had allowed her to quit selling office machinery and begin living what she had dreamed of years earlier: working to sell a worthy product she invented herself and having millions of people buy it.[1] And she had even appeared on Oprah!

But while Spanx's $20 Footless Body-Shaping Pantyhose had sold around thirty thousand units by January,[2] producing $400,000 in revenue,[3] those sales still represented a single product. The company itself was in its infancy, and it was still unproven.

Businessman and venture capitalist Kevin O'Leary, the self-proclaimed "Mr. Wonderful" on the ABC television show *Shark Tank*, probably would have told Sara at this point, "You're a product, not a company."[4] (Fortunately for her, the first time she would appear on *Shark Tank* was in 2017, several years in the future, and by then she was one of the sharks, not a contestant.) O'Leary has said the same thing to dozens of budding inventors. And he often explains that a single product, no matter how popular, does not always produce a scalable business. For example, regarding one product pitched on the show in 2013, he offered a royalty deal rather than a more-risky traditional investment. "Right now, what it does is it uses capital," he said. "It just sucks cash. The bigger you get, the more distribution you get, the more money you're gonna need."[5]

Luckily, Spanx had something else going for it: Sara's creative spirit and entrepreneurial drive. In 2015, Lori Greiner, another shark, expressed a different opinion on companies that start with a single product, when she spoke at an event hosted by Staples for its small business initiative. "If you have one genius product and good entrepreneurs, you can then turn that one product into a huge success," Greiner said. "And then of course continue to grow your business by creating other products, because you don't have to stop and be a one-hit wonder."[6] She wasn't describing Spanx or Sara, but she might as well have been. Spanx's advantage at the beginning of 2001 was Sara herself.

## Capitalizing on Her Strengths

Sales of the single Spanx product, Footless Body-Shaping Pantyhose, continued to grow steadily after the beginning of the year. By hiring a tiny staff and using the fulfillment company, Sara had gained breathing room, enabling her to get more sleep and have more time to think. And with that new freedom, she gave attention to the two things that she was very good at: creating new solutions to problems, and selling more product.

Sara didn't have to look far for product ideas. A self-described "recreational thinker," she had been making observations and wondering about new ways to do things for years. "I pay attention to things that haven't evolved and why," she once said of her hobby. "I ask myself questions all day, every day. I could be looking at a table and be like, 'Why is the table like that? When was the table first created? Is that the actual best design for a table? Or could there be something different?'"[7]

Because Sara carried a notebook everywhere, she always recorded her musings and big ideas. One of those ideas, a fairly simple variation on her original product, would become her second invention. The problem it would solve was in the design of fishnet pantyhose. A popular garment, often purchased by women who wanted to wear them with a little black dress for a nice evening out, fishnets looked very attractive on a woman's legs. To make the familiar mesh fishnet pattern, traditional hosiery companies had constructed them entirely of thick, crisscrossing threads, from waist to toe. But they came with a side effect that appeared when the pattern was stretched across a woman's upper thighs and bottom, especially under fitted or thin clothing: traditional fishnets tended to create a visible and unappealing latticework on the wearer's rear end.

Sara's solution to the problem was simple: attach the top portion of her Footless Body-Shaping Pantyhose (from waist to mid-thigh) to fishnet legs. (Unlike her original product, this one would also include feet.) In addition to eliminating the visible mesh and creating a clean look on the derriere, the

resulting design introduced Spanx's unique innovations to a
new garment. These fishnets promised to inspire confidence
in women through both attractive legs *and* a smooth, tight
bottom.

Just like her first Spanx product, Sara's second invention
ended up with a simple and descriptive name: Control-Top
Fishnets. And since these pantyhose had feet, which made
them much more familiar to shoppers, they needed less explanation than the footless ones had. But they still needed a slogan. Spanx had become a viable brand in the marketplace, in
spite of the mildly risqué name and "We've Got Your Butt Covered!" slogan. But it still danced on the line between appropriate and inappropriate in many minds. If Sara wanted to, she
could choose a slogan that leaned more toward appropriate.
"Classing things up" might widen the product's audience a little. But Sara continued dancing on the line. The slogan for
Product #2 was: "No More Grid Butt!"[8]

## Just Keep Selling

Sara's instincts informed more than the look of Spanx products. She also followed them in her next course of action. After
receiving more sales than she could handle from the endorsement of Oprah, who could reasonably be described as the number one influencer among women in the entire country, Sara
still didn't let up. Instead, she would do even more to get the
word out. So, she packed her bags, left behind her fledgling
company and staff, and went back on the road—visiting department stores all over the United States. To an outsider, this
might have looked like another unwise decision, but again, it
worked for Sara.

Based on what she'd learned so many years ago from Wayne Dyer's teaching, Sara was taking responsibility for her own happiness and success. That meant doing everything she was capable of. She later explained: "I am not going to let my success be contingent on other people."[9] For months, Sara personally stood in the aisles of a variety of distant department stores, hawking her Spanx. But even as she fearfully flew all over the United States, she kept in close contact with her team. She also came back to Atlanta as often as possible. And following her instincts bore fruit: her presence in the stores, explaining why women needed her invention, helped sell more Spanx. Word continued to spread.

One surprising response came from the stores' sales associates. Sara often met with store employees, helping them "get" what Spanx could do, and just connecting with them. And this turned them into a "sales force." Her time investment and ability to connect enchanted many hosiery department employees, who were soon rooting for her to succeed.[10]

## Meet Me in the Middle

When Sara originally approached Neiman Marcus, Saks, and Bloomingdale's, she was positioning her product with a specific audience. That continued as other high-end department stores came on board. Even Spanx's appearance among Oprah's favorite things in 2000 tended to appeal to shoppers who were comfortable with a higher price point. According to Wes Moss, Sara had an uncanny ability to start at the top, which meant that "her brand captured affluent customers, who generally have the most brand loyalty." Sara seemed to understand this instinctively as well. She said, "I know if you start at the high end, it's always easier to go down. But once you start in the middle market, it's almost impossible to go up."[11]

Even after Oprah Winfrey's powerful "blessing," Sara kept looking for ways to personally promote and sell her product to other audiences. Spanx, as a new invention that women didn't know they needed, seemed to sell better after Sara herself gave a personal explanation and demonstration. But going to one store at a time and talking with one woman at a time was not a fast or efficient way to build a huge following. She needed to expose Spanx to the largest possible audience at once.

It shouldn't be a surprise, then, that Sara started thinking about QVC, the shopping television network owned at the time by Comcast. A well-known fixture on cable TV across the country, QVC could promise millions of eyeballs to entrepreneurs who demonstrated their products on the show. In just a few minutes talking directly to the camera, Sara could connect with women all over the country and personally convince them that Spanx could change their lives. Of course, she applied for the show.

When Sara told her friends and advisers what she was doing, they worried that if the product was suddenly available for purchase in a less prestigious market than the high-end department stores, the company's reputation would suffer. And QVC was not just *slightly* less prestigious, like the lower-end department store J.C. Penney. With its twenty-four-hour infomercial format, the shopping channel had plenty of critics. Many consumers avoided it completely because they couldn't help associating it with wacky products and hucksters shouting, "But wait! There's more!"

Sara's friends pleaded with her not to go through with it. "Your brand is at Bergdorf Goodman and Neiman Marcus," they said. "You can't also sell on QVC. You'll kill your brand!"[12] But for someone like Sara, a shopping channel on TV was just a highly effective way to get the word out to the largest number of potential customers possible. "I chose QVC, and was very determined about it, because it was free advertising," she said. More than any magazine spread or radio ad, a personal appearance on QVC would allow her to demonstrate the product and almost completely control her message. This could be just like her department store visits, only with untold numbers of shoppers at a time.

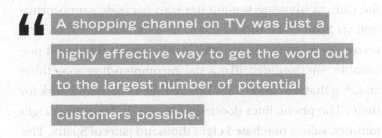

**A shopping channel on TV was just a highly effective way to get the word out to the largest number of potential customers possible.**

After all, Sara often said that Spanx was "an invention that needed explaining."[13] She could explain it to thousands of women at a time, helping them understand *why* they needed footless pantyhose.

## Not So Fast

As one of tens of thousands of annual applicants for QVC's product line, Sara's product went through a rigorous vetting process. Spanx passed the initial quality tests, and Vendor Relations Specialist Linda Simmons became a fan almost on a fluke. Simmons, who received between fifty and one hundred products per week, told the *Wall Street Journal* in 2003, "The sample she sent happened to be my size. I tried it, and that's all it took for me."[14]

At first, the QVC buyers were less enthusiastic. The shopping channel already offered a hosiery line, so they were reluctant to add another. But after four months and many phone conversations between Sara and Linda Simmons, the company eventually invited Sara to do a short segment on the program.

In May 2001, Sara introduced her product to the QVC audience on TV for the first time ever. In the amount of airtime that she was given, less than ten minutes, Sara spoke passionately to the camera, showing women her own backside's transformation via Spanx. She turned out to be a natural on TV, coming across as everyone's best friend. Authentically funny and personable, she sounded like a pal recommending something amazing that had worked for her that she knew would work for them. The phone lines flooded with calls. In fewer than eight minutes, callers purchased eight thousand pairs of Spanx. This was more than double QVC's initial order.[15]

> **In under eight minutes, callers purchased eight thousand pairs of Spanx.**

With that success, a beautiful relationship began between Sara and QVC, and she appeared frequently on the channel after that. In 2002, Spanx sales through QVC reached $8 million, representing approximately 30 percent of their revenue.[16]

"The momentum and the amount of product you can sell on QVC is mind-boggling," Sara said later. And again, she was proven right: the TV infomercial was a perfect medium for a product like Spanx and a sales professional like her.

## Good News and Bad News

In early 2001, the small Spanx team moved into their first actual office space. With all the selling that Sara was doing on the road, and then the huge success on QVC, keeping department store buyers happy and their shelves stocked with product was a challenge. Even with the help of the fulfillment company, the staff worked tirelessly to keep up.[17] At the same time, Sara was in the office less and less, and cracks were beginning to show.

More and more often, department store employees across the country had to apologize to disappointed customers when their supplies of Spanx ran low. One such shopper was Laurie Ann Goldman. A longtime executive with Coca-Cola in Atlanta, she was at the time the director of worldwide licensing for the brand.[18] She was also a new mother and eager to try out the smoothing and slimming qualities of Spanx post-childbirth. But when she visited her local Saks Fifth Avenue in search of Control-Top Fishnets, her size was completely sold out. Laurie Ann returned to the store several times, only to be met with frustration again and again. One day, after yet another apology from a sales associate, she told the young woman, "You really need to talk to your vendor about a replenishment plan."[19] Coincidentally, Sara's then-boyfriend, who was working at the time as the Spanx COO, was in the store and overheard the conversation. He exchanged numbers with Goldman.[20]

Sara's boyfriend returned to the office and told her about this very specific criticism from someone who seemed to know what she was talking about. And Sara's reaction, rather than taking offense, was to invite Laurie Ann out to lunch.

## The Gift of Perfect Timing

When the two women met, over lunch, Sara asked Laurie Ann what kind of "replenishment plan" they needed in order to keep products in stores. Laurie Ann responded with a description of what she would do if she were in Sara's situation. She went on to explain how to improve supply chain management and product replenishment. As Sara listened and learned, it seemed that Laurie Ann possessed great expertise and experience in something she herself knew very little about. Believing she could learn a lot from Laurie Ann, and following her instincts once again, Sara asked right then if she could hire her as a consultant. Laurie Ann agreed. Soon they were meeting regularly so Sara could learn from Laurie Ann on a regular basis.

Following Laurie Ann's advice, Sara and her team soon improved the supply chain process. But even as Sara's understanding of day-to-day operations increased, it became clear that logistics were never going to be an area of strength. Her expertise and passion lay elsewhere, which meant she could work hard to become an adequate manager, or she could hire someone more naturally suited for it. So Sara asked Laurie Ann if she would consider working for Spanx. And in 2002, Laurie Ann Goldman took the position of CEO of the company.[21]

According to Caroline Leahey, writing in *Fortune* magazine, Spanx "would never have hit icon status without CEO Goldman's focused vision."[22] And it does seem that Laurie Ann arrived as CEO at the perfect time for Sara and Spanx. With her greater understanding of operations and fulfillment, two areas that needed improvement, she was uniquely qualified to build a profitable and well-run company on the foundation of Sara's hosiery creativity.

Right away, the new CEO took over practical business decisions and day-to-day operations for the company. She immediately introduced much more formality and structure.[23] And soon, everything was running much more smoothly and systematically. With clearer deadlines, standards, and expectations, team members worked together more effectively and efficiently. They got more done with less effort and achieved their goals with greater accuracy and speed. And customers were no longer frustrated by product shortages in stores.

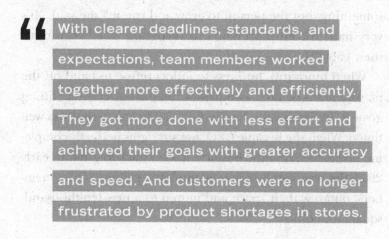

> With clearer deadlines, standards, and expectations, team members worked together more effectively and efficiently. They got more done with less effort and achieved their goals with greater accuracy and speed. And customers were no longer frustrated by product shortages in stores.

Goals became much more important with Laurie Ann's arrival. The new CEO was confident from the very beginning that Spanx was going to be huge. So she instituted formal business planning, including one-year and three-year targets. From her time at Coca-Cola, she also cared a great deal about the customer experience. While finding first-time customers was important, it wasn't enough to build Spanx into what she believed it could be. To create a world-class brand, they also needed to retain customers and give them reasons to recommend the products to others. Laurie Ann communicated that product quality was essential to this level of customer satisfaction. "Every time somebody puts on a Spanx product, one of two things can happen," she said. "Our brand can get stronger, or our brand can get weaker. We gain leverage or we lose leverage."[24]

No longer required to make every decision or figure out every process, Sara could continue selling—on the road and QVC—and rest assured that the company was running smoothly. She had even more freedom and time to think creatively as well. Sara later said her greatest decision was hiring a CEO. "As an entrepreneur, you are the person meant to start something, not the person to grow and run it," she said. "It's very hard for entrepreneurs to recognize this because it's their baby."[25]

When innovative business founders refuse to hand off the management of their companies, they often end up stifling growth. In Sara's case, Laurie Ann Goldman's arrival was well timed. When she became CEO, her strengths perfectly complemented Sara's. And the business was on track to grow. In early 2003, the company, which now employed eighteen team members, outgrew their space and moved to a new ten-thousand-square-foot office.[26]

## The Ideas Kept Coming

With all of her added thinking time, Sara kept coming up with product ideas. Soon after Laurie Ann joined the company in 2002, the third product, Power Panties, launched. Described as "the first legband-free, tummy-minimizing mid-thigh hosiery shaper," a pair of Power Panties extended from the waist to the middle of the thigh, looking a lot like an old-fashioned girdle. But Sara's new undergarment was thinner, cooler, and less constricting than any girdle ever made, because it was made from hosiery material. Like the other two Spanx products, Power Panties were seamless and designed to be worn alone, eliminating the need for other undergarments—and erasing the panty line as a result. Also continuing with her innovative manufacturing techniques, Sara eliminated a girdle's traditional elastic leg band. She replaced it with a softer, looser, and wider mid-thigh band made of the same hosiery material as the rest of the garment. This meant that it didn't create a bulge or dent on the thigh as old girdles did.

Power Panties greatly increased the market for Spanx, because they could be worn under much shorter garments. Sara had invented the original product to eliminate visible panty lines and cellulite *under slacks*, not necessarily skirts or dresses. But now, women could wear Spanx with even more of the clothing in their closets. Understandably, Power Panties were popular from the beginning, and they eventually sold more on a consistent basis than the first product. Of course, after her original huge success on QVC, Sara made another appearance on the channel to promote Power Panties, selling eight thousand units in only *six* minutes.[27]

Mama Spanx maternity products also launched in 2002. Though at that time Sara herself had never been pregnant, this line of products was designed to solve several problems with traditional manufacturers' maternity pantyhose, rather than to hide a pregnancy or shrink a woman's size. Old maternity pantyhose tended to bind, sag, and/or stretch out. Plus, they did nothing to eliminate panty lines. With smoothing and shaping effects limited to the thighs and rear, and a belly panel that stretched to fit every stage of pregnancy, Mama Spanx eliminated panty lines and helped pregnant women feel more confident. Plus, they enabled women to buy fewer pairs of maternity undergarments because they would fit for all nine months. Expectant mothers and their doctors were especially pleased with Mama Spanx belly and back support, which helped relieve back pain.

## Moving Up and to the Right

The combination of Sara's creativity and Laurie Ann's efficient handling of daily operations created a steep and consistent growth trajectory for Spanx. They kept adding accounts and were now in most high-end department stores. QVC sales kept growing. And direct-to-consumer online sales were expanding at a steady rate.

In 2003, Spanx launched in the United Kingdom as the very first body-shaping product constructed out of hosiery to be sold in that country. British women remembered old-fashioned binding girdles, too, and they loved the comfort of Spanx. Later that same year, Sara appeared on TV overseas, pitching her products on both QVC UK (with an average audience of 11.6 million viewers) and QVC Germany (viewed by 34 million on average).[28] Spanx continued to sell the most by far in the United States, but the market in Europe grew steadily in 2003. That year, in only its third full year of selling product, the company earned $31 million worldwide.[29]

Product development in 2003 and 2004 was really humming along for the Spanx team. As revenue increased, they poured profits back into the company, designing and launching more new products. What had begun as Sara alone in a small apartment was now a team of twenty-four people, all but three of them women,[30] who participated in a high-energy, fun, and collaborative process.[31]

" Product development in 2003 and 2004 was really humming along for the Spanx team. As revenue increased, they poured profits back into the company, designing and launching more new products. What had begun as Sara alone in a small apartment was now a team of twenty-four people, all but three of them women.

And with every new prototype, team members gathered to test it on real women—usually starting with Sara herself. Still shunning the plastic mannequin method of testing that Sara had seen in traditional hosiery factories, the team always sought feedback from real people on each product's comfort as well as its visual effect. Testers soon got used to standing around in undergarments, being poked and prodded and asked to spin or face the other direction. Sara and her team even brought in friends, family members, and others to evaluate each product and give their input. Sara's mother and grandmother often joined in. The development team paid close attention to the feedback and made changes as many times as needed to get the product right.

Product development was never-ending from 2001 to 2008. In the company's first four years, it ideated, designed, tested, refined, and launched over forty new garments. But they were just getting started. Sara never stopped jotting down problems that needed solutions in a notebook every day, and soon had dozens filled and stacked in her office. She and the team continuously mined her notebooks for new great ideas and solutions. Garments that solved problems for women kept coming. And when Target requested Spanx shaping ingenuity at a lower price point, the team designed and launched a new line called Assets by Spanx, which sold well not only in the US, but also overseas. By the end of 2008, the Spanx catalog contained more than two hundred different items.

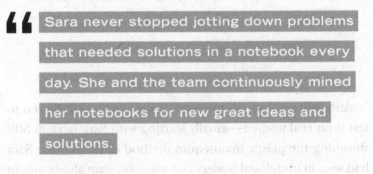

> Sara never stopped jotting down problems that needed solutions in a notebook every day. She and the team continuously mined her notebooks for new great ideas and solutions.

## ▪ LESSON WE CAN LEARN FROM THE SPANX STORY: SHARPEN YOUR THINKING SKILLS

Thinking is a skill, and it takes time and effort to learn. "Throughout school we spend so much time being taught things like geometry, trigonometry, algebra and history," Sara once said. "All of that is really interesting and important, but nobody really teaches you how to think. So you have to take it upon yourself to be your own teacher, in order to reach your potential."[32] What are you doing to intentionally sharpen your thinking skills?

The most popular of the dozens of new products launched was the Bra-llelujah, so named after a female staffer's husband thought of it—while sitting in church. Yes, the funny names continued. This product solved another problem that Sara had observed, this time in bras. The traditional garment was constructed using several elastic bands, sometimes even crisscrossing across the chest. (This was actually promoted as a selling point in the old "Cross Your Heart" bra TV commercials.) The elastic, which was often stretched tightly on the back, tended to press deeply and uncomfortably into the skin. The thick bands also showed through most shirts, and the closure created a bump for the wearer to feel when she leaned back into a chair. Furthermore, the bands often squeezed so hard that they emphasized what Sara referred to as "unsightly back fat" above and below them. Sara and her team designed the Bra-llelujah with a front closure and a back made entirely of hosiery material—with zero elastic. It was soft and comfortable enough to wear all day. And because it lay smooth across the back, it eliminated the problems of lines, bumps, and back fat.

## A Famous Flashpoint

Even as the product line increased, so did another phenomenon that no one had predicted: showing off Spanx in public became even more trendy. Shapewear seemed to be turning into a badge of honor. No surprise in America, with its celebrity and movie star obsession, the flashing trend began on Hollywood red carpets, when the stars finally revealed their "secret." This seems to have started in 2003, when Gwyneth Paltrow cheerfully volunteered in an interview that she had worn two pairs of Spanx under her form-fitting gown on the red carpet right after the birth of her first child.[33] She also gushed, "It's how all the Hollywood girls do it!"

Soon afterward, Oprah Winfrey shared with her TV audience that she'd "given up regular panties" and wore only Spanx under everything.[34] This additional plug from Oprah sealed the deal. As Louise France wrote in England's the *Guardian* in 2008, Oprah's seal of approval was "pretty much like God putting Power Panties on his Christmas list."[35]

Steadily, more stars admitted to Spanxing. Early adopters (and admitters!) included Jessica Alba ("I wore Spanx before anyone. Spanx are the only thing that smooths out all of my lumps and bumps.") and Tyra Banks ("Every celebrity walking down the red carpet. You think she's all just naturally like 'shooop.' A lot of them have Spanx on. You put 'em on, it sucks you up, baby. No matter what red carpet, I got 'em on.").[36] When asked on the red carpet "who" they were wearing, dozens of actresses mentioned—*and thanked*—Spanx right along with their dress designer. The cat came completely out of the bag in October 2006, when *In Touch Weekly* published a breathless article/exposé revealing Spanx as "Hollywood's Big Secret."[37]

From then on, almost "all the Hollywood girls" were not only wearing Spanx, they were crediting it with their smooth and sleek appearance. They often lifted a hemline to show them off. All these famous women in Spanx offered the world visible evidence of what the products could do to a woman's figure under fitted garments. Spanx appeared in public more and more, peeking out in paparazzi photos and on TV appearances. No matter how tight the garment, every star began to look smooth, sleek, and toned underneath.

## Spanx Was Ahead of the Curve(s)

It didn't hurt that fashion was experiencing a transformation in the early 2000s. Garments were indeed becoming more form-fitting, but they were also changing shape. The hourglass figure regained popularity. The grunge and heroin chic of the 1990s appeared to be officially dead with the release of the 2001 Destiny's Child hit single "Bootylicious." The song, with Beyoncé singing lead vocals and popularizing a word coined by rapper Snoop Dogg in 1992, rocketed to number one on the US pop charts. By 2004, women everywhere wanted to be "bootylicious." That June, *Atlanta* magazine published a profile by Candice Dyer with this clear description of how Spanx benefited from this culture shift:

> While Spanx owes its success to Blakely's inventiveness and persistence, it also has enjoyed good timing, stepping out to the cultural bass-beat of "Baby Got Back." Every era anoints an It Girl, and Jennifer Lopez was starting to shake her callipygian assets [i.e., well-shaped buttocks] (rumored to be insured for $1 million) to mass-media domination when Spanx got its footing. American beauty standards seem to be shifting away from the anorexic, Barbie doll look toward the shapely, fly flesh of hip-hop videos. From low-riding jeans to an increasing demand for gluteal implants, we are a nation that worships the "bootylicious."[38]

As 2004 drew to a close, the "booty" was indeed the fashion focus. Spanx, which had focused on women's "booties" since 2000, was mainstream. Sara's risqué product name was no longer considered inappropriate. With every product, Sara and Spanx now were on the leading edge of a massive curve. After all, in addition to offering women a firm, smooth, and lineless booty, Sara's inventions had always showcased it. And later even enhanced it. Products came out that were specifically designed "to avoid the flat, uni-butt look that many shapers give your backside."[39]

Spanx rode the wave of making women's curves look amazing throughout the early 2000s. After earning $4 million in their first year and $10 million in their second,[40] Spanx sales steadily increased year after year: $31 million in 2003,[41] $40 million in 2004, roughly $80 million in 2005,[42] and $150 million in 2006.[43] In the next two years after that, they shot up even faster, reaching $350 million in 2008.[44] Some women became obsessed with the product. *Glamour* magazine editor Suze Yalof Schwartz called Spanx "hosiery crack."[45] The shapewear wave was showing no sign of ebbing. And even though the major hosiery manufacturers were quickly launching their own versions of updated shapewear, Spanx remained the best seller.[46]

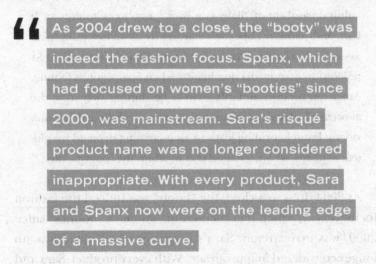

As 2004 drew to a close, the "booty" was indeed the fashion focus. Spanx, which had focused on women's "booties" since 2000, was mainstream. Sara's risqué product name was no longer considered inappropriate. With every product, Sara and Spanx now were on the leading edge of a massive curve.

## Making the Most of Every Connection

Spanx the company was rolling. And so was Sara. She gained a model and a mentor in 2004 when she auditioned to be a contestant on a reality show called *The Rebel Billionaire* featuring England's Sir Richard Branson, the unconventional billionaire owner of the Virgin Group. She got on the show and met challenge after challenge as other contestants were eliminated. She even made it all the way to the finale, but was chosen as runner-up. As part of that experience, she got the opportunity to travel to South Africa and spend time with Nelson Mandela.

Sara also got to experience her dream come true. Back in 2000 when Spanx was first featured on *The Oprah Winfrey Show*, she didn't get to go to Chicago or meet Oprah. But in 2007, Sara was finally invited to sit down face-to-face with Oprah on her show.

There was one other significant connection that occurred during this season of Spanx's success. In 2006, Sara was invited to take part in a charity poker tournament in Las Vegas, hosted by Marquis Jet, a company that leases private planes. By that time, she had become a loyal customer because of her fear of flying. She said that, at least in a private plane, if she had a panic attack, she could ask the pilot to land.

At the event, she hit it off with the Marquis Jet cofounder Jesse Itzler when they chatted about their similar lack of skill in playing poker. Within a year, they were dating, and in 2007, they moved into a Manhattan apartment together. Jesse, a former rapper (with the prescient 1992 hit "Shake It [Like a White Girl]"), was based in New York City, where he founded and ran several successful ventures. The pair, both high-energy, positive, and funny, were engaged in 2008. Sara had only the briefest of second thoughts when she realized that Jesse might not be aware of exactly how wealthy she was. At dinner a month before the wedding, she brought up the awkward topic.

"I think I make more money than you think I do," she said. Jesse just smiled at her and replied, "It couldn't have happened to a nicer person."[47] They married on a Florida beach in October of 2008. Their first child, Lazer, would be born in 2009.

At this point, Sara had a family. She had mentors. She was independently wealthy. She was the 100 percent owner of a thriving business. She had invented its products, just as she dreamed. She had grown her staff to more than forty-five employees, who worked collaboratively in their bright and airy ten-thousand-square-foot office. And she had hired a CEO to help her run the business.

No longer just a single novelty product, Spanx was the real deal. First to market, Spanx *was* modern shapewear in the minds of the public. Sara and company were on top, and it appeared like they would stay there for the foreseeable future. But in business, things don't always go as planned.

## ▪ LESSON WE CAN LEARN FROM THE SPANX STORY: WHO CAN HELP YOU?

No one becomes successful on her own. Great companies are not built by a single individual. Sara was willing to admit that she needed help. When someone criticized how she and her staff were doing things, she didn't get defensive. She asked if the critic wanted a job. Who do you know who might be able to help you improve yourself, your product (or service), your team, or your processes? If you can, enlist them. If you can't enlist them, learn from them.

"Just because you are CEO, don't think you have landed. You must continually increase your learning, the way you think, and the way you approach the organization. I've never forgotten that."

—INDRA NOOYI,
Business Executive and Former CEO of Pepsico

## CHAPTER SEVEN

# GROWING PAINS

I n mid-2011, Sara heard from Clare O'Connor with *Forbes* magazine, asking for an interview for a story. Sara loved *Forbes*. They'd given her and Spanx valuable coverage in the past. But life was crazy now. She was working to weigh every interview request before immediately saying yes. But when O'Connor explained the purpose of the interview, it became clear that it was worth doing. She heard, "We'd like to do a cover story on you for the March 2012 special issue." Certainly, Sara was listening intently after that. Then O'Connor revealed the theme of the entire issue: the Forbes Annual World Billionaires List. Sara Blakely was being added to the list because they had recently calculated her net worth at *one billion dollars*.

Earlier in 2011, four different Wall Street investment banks had valued Spanx at an average of one billion dollars. Then *Forbes*, with the help of industry analysts, corroborated that number and agreed. And because Sara remained the sole proprietor of the private company, a billion-dollar valuation for Spanx meant that *Sara was now considered a billionaire.*[1]

O'Connor wanted to interview Sara Blakely because she was now one of the "1,226 richest people on the planet."[2] Plus, she had *earned* 100 percent of her wealth—without the help of a husband or an inheritance. This made Sara, at forty-one, *the youngest self-made female billionaire in the world.*[3]

> **"** This made Sara, at forty-one, *the youngest self-made female billionaire in the world.*

## From Beach Bum to Billionaire— the Real Story!

Sara participated in what turned out to be multiple interviews with O'Connor, starting in the summer of 2011.[4] In addition to recording hours of conversations with Sara in the Spanx offices in Atlanta, the *Forbes* writer also spoke with Sara's husband, Jesse, in his New York office.

After the March 2012 issue of *Forbes* was published, suddenly everyone was clamoring to talk to "Sara Blakely, Youngest Self-Made Female Billionaire." *Time* soon named her one of 2012's most influential people. *Fortune* interviewed her. *Vogue* did a piece on her personal sense of fashion. And her story appeared on all the major US television networks. Even journalists in the United Kingdom took note, featuring her in publications like the *Daily Mail* and the *Guardian*.

In every feature on her, Sara charmed reporters and audiences alike. Her persona—blonde, pretty, funny, and enthusiastic—made her an entertaining subject. Cheerfully, she made herself available, welcoming reporter after reporter to tour the Spanx offices and even her home. She also posed gamely for dozens and dozens of photos. Viewers and readers alike enjoyed her stories of failure and success.

As always, Sara used her own story to point her audience toward her company and its products. Everything about her expressed her passion for helping women, along with her avid belief that her inventions would make their lives better. And yet, every report on Sara in 2012 seemed to be based on the same dozen questions—always focused on the birth and early years of her company. Everyone wanted to know as much as possible of *Sara's* story. After all, she had achieved "The American Dream." People were interested in how she did it.

Sara's face and personal history were all over the news, as people learned all about how "the young saleswoman from a Florida beach town had turned five thousand dollars into a billion." The story of the first decade of Spanx, from Sara's 1998 "aha" moment until about 2008, became so well known during that time that it was soon part of business lore.

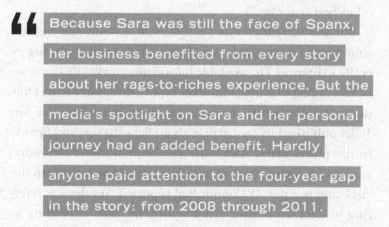

Because Sara was still the face of Spanx, her business benefited from every story about her rags-to-riches experience. But the media's spotlight on Sara and her personal journey had an added benefit. Hardly anyone paid attention to the four-year gap in the story: from 2008 through 2011.

Because Sara was still the face of Spanx, her business benefited from every story about her rags-to-riches experience. But the media's spotlight on Sara and her personal journey "from beach bum to billionaire" had an added benefit. Hardly anyone paid attention to the four-year gap in the story: from 2008 through 2011.

## Best Year Ever . . . ?

The *Forbes* story that launched the media cavalcade appeared on newsstands in March of 2012. Of course, it would have been written and submitted months earlier, probably during the last quarter of 2011. So it's fairly safe to assume that the financial figures mentioned by the writer, Clare O'Connor, were obtained or calculated sometime in 2011. This is important, because along with a $1 billion valuation for Spanx, O'Connor also mentioned that the company was estimated to be earning "just south of $250 million in revenue." Then, near the very end of the article, she also mentioned that Spanx was "coming off its best year ever."[5]

But was it, really? Was $250 million actually the highest amount that Spanx had earned in annual revenue, during its entire existence? The available information makes this unclear. But according to at least one other report, the answer is no. Only twelve months before the *Forbes* piece was published, the *New Yorker* published its own article about Sara Blakely and Spanx. In the piece, writer Alexandra Jacobs mentioned a revenue amount for Spanx that was at least *$100 million higher* than the 2011 number that O'Connor had reported. Yet she was referring to data from three years before, in 2008. According to Jacobs, Spanx's global retail sales for 2008 were *$350 million*.[6]

One possible explanation for the discrepancy is the difference between privately owned companies and those that are publicly traded. Public companies—such as competitors Maidenform and Hanes—are required to follow strict rules on reporting financial data. Accurate information is expected by stockholders and required by the stock market. Privately held companies like Spanx, on the other hand, are not held to the same reporting standards. They certainly can publish regular financial reports, but they are not required to. Nor are they required to back up their assertions with validated data. Private companies are able to keep their information private.

For an article or feature on a privately held company, financial data, such as revenue, may need to be discovered and validated in other ways. The simplest method is often for the reporter to ask the CEO or another executive at the company. But the company's leaders have a choice—not only in whether they release a number, but also in the exact number they release. Their numbers aren't usually wildly "off," because even though the data is hard to fact-check, it can be analyzed. That's what *Forbes* did (by consulting expert analysis) to conclude that Spanx and therefore Sara were worth $1 billion. What is not obvious is how *Forbes* verified the $250 million revenue figure for the same time period. As for Jacobs in the *New Yorker,* it's most likely that she asked a Spanx representative for a revenue amount, and she received the most recent information that they were willing or able to share: the 2008 figure of $350 million.[7]

## Other Possible Explanations

Of course, $250 million in revenue as reported in *Forbes* is nothing to sneeze at, and those earnings still enabled Sara to reach their billionaires list. But a difference of $100 million does brings to mind other questions. It's fairly clear from what we know that the company experienced rapid and steady growth through 2008. But if the above revenue numbers of $350 and $250 million are correct, sales seem to have leveled off and then trended down for a period of time. The good news was that sales stopped their slide at $250 million. But they seemed to remain flat. According to Spanx reports, until the end of 2014, revenue would remain flat at around $250 million.[8] Spanx's growth seems to have stalled. Why?

## After the Honeymoon

The answer to that question may begin with Sara's wedding day back in October 2008. Reciting her vows did a great deal more than make her a "Missus." With that step, she entered a season of family life that would divide her focus in new ways. It would also distance her not only mentally but physically from her company. Several events marked the change over the next few years.

Unsurprisingly, in early 2009, Sara and Jesse established their first home as a married couple. But the location may be surprising. They decided their "home base" would be in a condo overlooking Central Park in Manhattan. And Sara had to adjust to living hundreds of miles from her company headquarters. At first, she traveled back and forth as frequently as possible, and mostly kept her head in the details of running the company. Until the next event . . .

Sara was pregnant for the first half of the year. And that summer, she and Jesse welcomed their firstborn son and named him Lazer, an old family name. As a first-time mother of a newborn, Sara had to devote the majority of her time and energy to learning how to be a parent. Like many new mothers, she considered herself unprepared, saying later that she didn't know what she was doing at first because, "You haven't been training for it."[9] And as any parent knows, during those first few sleepless and chaotic months of motherhood, Sara would have little time or mental energy left over for Spanx. Right after Lazer's birth, she had to pause her trips back and forth to Atlanta. Once he grew past the infant stage, she did resume her travels, often arriving in the offices with him on her hip. But after the onset of parenthood, no one's life ever returns to its previous "normal." Instead, a new normal begins.

## Equilibrium

From 2009 through early 2013, Sara and Laurie Ann Goldman established the new normal for their company. As Lazer grew older, and Sara increased her trips into the office, she was able to touch base more easily with Laurie Ann and other management staff. She also jumped back into product testing and brainstorming sessions. And as Laurie Ann managed daily operations while Sara was not in Atlanta, Sara became an idea-generating machine. Making the best of her lengthened commute—two nerve-wracking hours in the air, each way—she declared that all the extra travel gave her the time and solitude to think up new products for Spanx. Notebooks full of ideas were soon stacked all over her office.

From the beginning, she and Jesse seemed well suited for each other. Years later, they agreed that marrying the right person made the difference. They described it as the decision that had made the most impact on their lives, especially as entrepreneurs.[10] "We respect that each of us moves at a fast pace," said Sara. "That might bother some, but we get it."[11] Their high energy levels and remarkable tolerance for risk melded well together.

## It's the Economy, Stupid

Sara's new season as a wife and mother created temporary challenges for Spanx, which everyone worked to manage. But another factor beyond the company's control—the global financial crisis and the Great Recession—had officially begun in late 2007. With the stock market crash in 2008, the overall decline accelerated. And even though the recession was officially considered over at the end of 2009, its effects in the United States continued.

Even after the foreclosure rate finally peaked at the end of 2010,[12] the country felt its effects for the next few years. And the resulting feelings of economic insecurity made people cautious with their money. So many had watched their homes and retirement funds plunge in value that it would take time for overall confidence to return. In the meantime, with low consumer confidence came low consumer spending. And this was especially true for most products that would be considered indulgences and luxuries. Many consumers hunkered down to wait out the poor economy, and postponed purchasing nonnecessities in the meantime.

Despite all of Sara's sales ability, few consumers would have considered a pair of Spanx a necessity. So this was the real reason for their revenue slowdown during that same period, right? The answer is yes, but to a limited degree. The slow economy had to have some impact, but it was perhaps not as great as some might think.

This may seem counterintuitive, since the fashion and apparel industries are usually among the hardest hit when consumer spending decreases, but Spanx actually *benefited* from the downturn at first. The economic trend responsible for this strange phenomenon was observed during the hard financial times in the United States during World War II. After noticing that certain categories of consumer goods seemed immune to economic swings, financial scholars tried to discover why. After some analysis, they observed that the products in question had two things in common: they were relatively inexpensive, and purchasing them seemed to give the buyer a big emotional boost. In other words, they offered a way to feel *a lot* better for *a little bit* of money. These items offered "more bang for the buck," so shoppers kept spending the "buck" to get the "bang." In fact, sales numbers in these categories actually tended to increase, even as spending in most other categories decreased. Scholars in the 1940s referred to them as "affordable indulgences."[13]

After the October 2008 stock market crash when consumer spending plunged in almost every category, experts once again reported on the "affordable indulgence" trend. Customers continued spending on certain products. But a new product appeared on their lists: hosiery. Spending on hosiery actually increased at the beginning of the recession. Writer Cheryl Tan, in a November 2008 article for the *Wall Street Journal*, theorized that hosiery was becoming the new "affordable indulgence." She called it "the hosiery index," noting that online retailer BareNecessities.com (a big Spanx vendor) had seen hosiery sales "increase 60% in September and 70% in October," the month that the stock market crashed. And regarding Spanx in particular, Bare Necessities data from January through October 31 of 2008—before the crash but after the recognized 2007 start of the recession—showed Spanx sales were also up, with as much as a 77 percent increase—in patterned tights—compared to the same period the previous year.[14] However, while Spanx did benefit at least a little bit from the "hosiery index," they still lost $100 million in revenue during the recession years. The economic downturn clearly deserves some of the blame—but probably not all of it—for where they found themselves in 2011.

## Competition Didn't Help

As first to market back in 2000, Spanx had defined the modern shapewear category. But competitors soon emerged, and by 2009, they had flooded the shapewear market. The company still represented the category in many minds, similar to Kleenex. But while women might be thinking "Spanx" as they shopped, they now had many brands to choose from in the growing shapewear section of their local store. Even Spanx's red packages with their cheeky names didn't stand out as much, since other companies had long ago copied Sara's preference for bright colors and clever marketing. In 2011, when discussing a package redesign, Sara would comment on the challenge, "Now that everyone has copied us so much, it feels stale."[15]

Sara was probably on to something. Spanx could have become old news. And with so many other brands to choose from, shoppers could afford to be picky. Different brands even emphasized different features, with some promising greater comfort, while others showed off a sexier silhouette or a more personalized fit. And the wide variety of price points—possibly the most important feature during a recession—would have a significant effect on Spanx. The first brand to offer shapewear "by women, for women" still delivered on their promise of high quality and durability. But those still came with a price tag on the higher end. Now, with all the different price points offered by the competition, the good news for consumers was that almost anyone could afford shapewear. The bad news for Sara's company was that they didn't all choose Spanx.

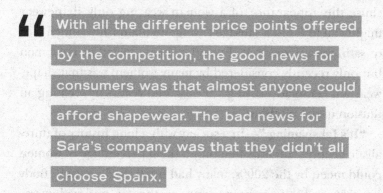

> With all the different price points offered by the competition, the good news for consumers was that almost anyone could afford shapewear. The bad news for Sara's company was that they didn't all choose Spanx.

## Perception Mattered

During the same period, as shapewear became old news, the excitement about what one woman had called "Mannequin Ass" in 2007 began to fade. Now, the newness had worn off, and consumers considered Spanx and its imitators more objectively. Some comments became louder. They included . . .

**"This is really uncomfortable."**—From women after a few years of regular use. Sara's inventions, with their modifications designed "by women for women," were an improvement in comfort than an old-fashioned girdle. But most women would admit that wearing them could be compared to wearing a wetsuit. And God forbid if a woman in shapewear had to use the restroom in a hurry. Pulling the garment down the lower half of the body was a task best handled slowly and carefully. When bunched around the ankles, the garment would act as a band holding them firmly together, creating an equilibrium problem. Then, pulling everything back up the torso and into place took even longer.

**"It's not sexy."**—From women and men, and not just because the appearance of a woman wearing only shapewear might call to mind a sausage casing, no matter how much lace or satin was affixed to it. The other issue, voiced by most men but only recently considered by many women, was that shapewear was "false advertising." It obscured reality by creating an illusion under clothing.

**"It's fat shaming."**—In a society with a long history of unrealistic beauty standards that only a small percentage of women could meet, by the 2000s, many had finally had enough. Body positivity and self-acceptance were on the rise, and society was starting to reject comments or advertising that even hinted that to be overweight was bad, ugly, or something to hide or be ashamed of. Back in 2004, Dove—a brand mostly associated with soap—had brought attention to new attitudes with its "Real Beauty" ad campaign. The first ads featured images of women in their undergarments, with a variety of body sizes and types, all of them larger than a size 0 model. At the time, it was considered revolutionary, but received positively overall. The executives at lingerie maker Victoria's Secret (all male) reacted derisively. Plus, they launched a tone-deaf ad campaign of their own, known as "Perfect Body." It featured their bevy of supermodels, who were known as "Angels"—and rail-thin. Consumer response was swift and harsh, and the campaign was abruptly scrapped. By 2008, consumers' reaction tended to be negative toward any product that promised to make a woman look thinner, since the promise itself implied that thinner was good, and fat was bad.

**"It's a tool of the patriarchy."**—From feminist activists at first, but the general population was beginning to embrace this idea by the early teens. It emerged from questions about the definition of *beauty*. Defined for centuries by what most men considered attractive, the standard had been enforced by the fashion industry by corsets and other contraptions designed to change the shape of the female body. Specific trends went in and out of fashion. But in every era except perhaps the "let it all hang out" sixties, it seemed that the shape of women's clothing, and the contraptions and contortions she had to endure to wear it, were based on how a man felt about it, rather than how a woman felt in it. Modern shapewear, just like a whalebone corset or a wire bustle, modified—by force—a woman's body. Sure, Sara Blakely had introduced some modifications that made it more comfortable, but most women only wore it because of fashion's dictates. The dream Sara had stated in an interview in 2004, of "making the world a better place, one butt at a time," had begun to ring hollow in many ears.[16]

Tellingly, Spanx seemed to recognize and respond to some of the perception complaints. Their biggest changes were made to address the accusations of fat shaming or capitalizing on women's insecurities. The packaging and marketing copy for Spanx products made a gradual and subtle shift to emphasize "smoothing" and "shaping" over "slimming."

## Creativity versus Viability

Based on the article by Alexandra Jacobs for the *New Yorker*, Spanx had sold tens of millions of products around the world by 2010. The lifetime sales numbers at that time for their first two products alone totaled fifteen million. That equaled nine million pairs of footless pantyhose and six million of power panties. "The line is sold in thirty countries," Jacobs wrote, "and at more than ten thousand retail locations in the United States." Spanx also employed more than one hundred people.[17]

In New York, Sara was busy filling notebooks with ideas, which she would pitch to the team in Atlanta as often as she could. And the creativity showed no sign of slowing; new categories were introduced to the product list all the time, including legwear ("Tight-End Tights") and "In It to Slim It" activewear. The company even offered a high-end line of lacy lingerie called Haute Contour, and had just launched Spanx for Men. With more than two hundred different products in 2010, some Spanx executives had begun to worry, wrote Jacobs, that shoppers might have a hard time distinguishing between all of them.[18]

Spanx was flush with ideas, along with expertise in marketing and positioning. But how many variations on shapewear did they need to offer? Two hundred products might be overkill, hinting at a need for more focus in both idea generation and selection of the most viable ideas to implement. Creatives often come up with an abundance of wild ideas; that's actually the value they bring to the process. The greater the number of outlandish ideas, the greater the likelihood of discovering the one that will create a splash in the marketplace. It's possible that Spanx headquarters had become imbalanced, with more emphasis on creativity than on viability.

A rare entrepreneur, Sara had been able at the beginning to both create ideas and produce a finished product. She generated ideas that were so creative that they seemed impossible. Yet from 1998 through 2000, she created a plan, found the best contractors, convinced them of the viability of the idea, supervised the process, and ended up with physical products. And her products offered every feature she'd imagined, at the highest quality, and at the lowest possible cost. Then she turned around and sold them like crazy. And the company grew until it outgrew Sara.

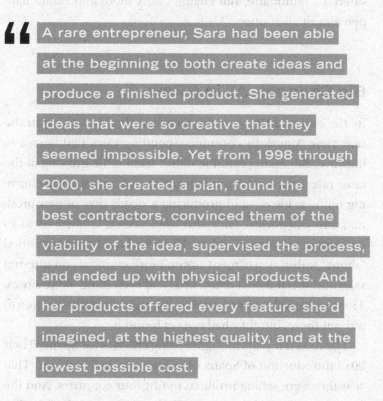

> A rare entrepreneur, Sara had been able at the beginning to both create ideas and produce a finished product. She generated ideas that were so creative that they seemed impossible. Yet from 1998 through 2000, she created a plan, found the best contractors, convinced them of the viability of the idea, supervised the process, and ended up with physical products. And her products offered every feature she'd imagined, at the highest quality, and at the lowest possible cost.

Laurie Ann Goldman's arrival as CEO in 2002 had allowed Spanx to leap to another level, and it just kept climbing—until the recession. By hiring a CEO, Sara could step back and focus more on creativity. Laurie Ann would be responsible for viability and implementation. Until 2009, the system seemed to work well. Yes, their catalog might have contained too many products. And Sara's frequent absences would have made it more difficult to maintain her creative synergy with Laurie Ann. But, overall, Spanx had survived an economic collapse. Now all they had to do was find a way to grow again. Around a year after *Forbes* had celebrated Sara's billionaire status, she was still considered a billionaire. But changes were afoot and would happen almost all at once.

## Big Changes, All in a Row

By the end of 2012, with the recession slowly receding in the rear view, American consumer spending rates had begun to improve. But Spanx revenue didn't seem to be growing at the same rate. Sara and Laurie Ann and their team were still churning out new ideas—and producing a steady flow of new products and categories. They also tried several creative ideas to encourage consumers to buy. These included Spanx-branded "shops" within department stores, more emphasis on internet sales and social media marketing, and even stand-alone stores. They expressed confidence that the right formula for growth was out there, but they had not yet found it.

The next few years brought several changes for Spanx. Their 2013 introduction of Spanx blue jeans was well received. That year they were selling products in fifty-four countries. And the staff, numbering 162, worked collaboratively in a colorful office space, which writer Alexandra Jacobs compared to "a hygienic bordello." Sara's touch was all over the décor, designed with comfort and fun in mind. Think cozy velvet sofas, pink shag carpeting, mirrors, and neon accents.

As for Sara herself, her presence in the office became even more rare after she became pregnant again in late 2013. This time it was *twins*. The following June, the Itzler family would increase by two: healthy baby boys named Lincoln and Charlie. Sara and Jesse would be trying to manage twin babies plus a preschooler. Again, family would have to take precedence over company for Sara. But she would find herself juggling more than she might have initially expected.

In February, just a few months before the Itzlers welcomed their sons, a transition at Spanx had unfolded: the company and Laurie Ann Goldman announced that they would part ways. No reason for the departure was offered; however, we can speculate on a few factors. For one thing, Laurie Ann was, above all, a branding expert. Her past experience in marketing for Coca-Cola had prepared her to build Spanx into a massive brand. And that emphasis on marketing and brand-building dovetailed nicely with Sara's. For years, as the two women built the brand together, they also built an incredibly successful business. More than a decade later, the brand and name recognition for Spanx were well established. Perhaps the business had moved beyond the building stage and Laurie Ann was departing to build something else. She seemed to say as much in an interview soon after her departure: "I have always gravitated towards positions where I can build something."[19]

Another possibility is that it was time for the next level of innovation and creativity. In the early years, Laurie Ann had supported Sara's creativity and out-of-the-box thinking by creating systems and processes to ensure quality and customer satisfaction. Sara and Laurie Ann were very knowledgeable about fashion and apparel—but as *consumers*. They had learned even more over the years of building the brand. But perhaps it was time for apparel expertise to increase within the leadership team now that operations were much larger and more complex. By bringing in experts in the industry, the company would certainly benefit from their knowledge. This would keep them from learning lessons the hard way, like the one Laurie Ann described in her talk for a conference seven months after her departure.

Years before, the Spanx team, after deciding to introduce a swimwear line, had worked for months to design and manufacture swimsuits that incorporated their famous smoothing technology. The suits were in stock and ready to be shipped when a retailer called to request their results after chlorine testing. Unaware of this standard test, which determined how well garments performed in a swimming pool, the Spanx team had not included it in their process. So they scrambled to solve the problem, according to Laurie Ann. She went on to describe her creative—and ultimately effective—solution: she took a sampling of Spanx suits to her home, then submerged them in her own swimming pool for a week.[20]

While the swimsuit story ended happily, it certainly introduced chaos and anxiety right before a product launch. With some changes to include more apparel manufacturing experts, Spanx could avoid similar experiences.

## The Season of Change

Included in the February 2014 announcement about Laurie Ann, Sara appointed an interim CEO: Gregg Ribatt. An apparel executive based in Boston, he had already been advising Sara. He would take over and assist her in finding his permanent replacement.[21]

Another big change came for Sara and Spanx in the first half of 2014. Sara and her husband listed the Manhattan apartment for sale. And she and her family soon moved to Atlanta. In June, Sara gave birth to her two sons. Only a month after that, Spanx hired Jan Singer as its new CEO.

## Culture, According to Sara Blakely

Once again living in the same city as her company, Sara would be able to instill her version of company culture more deeply into Spanx. The culture of Spanx at the very beginning was based on Sara's own personal values and beliefs. These included encouraging people, showing kindness, and embracing failure to learn from it. With a motivational leadership style, she motivated staff to want to give their best, encouraging them to take risks and overcome their fear of failure. One way she did this was through what she called "oops" meetings, where the stated purpose was for everyone, beginning with Sara, to share their own failures and "oops moments," preferably as funny stories. The colorful office environment was also challenging and fun whenever she was involved. Sara even required new employees to participate in stand-up comedy training to get past a fear of public speaking. Sara loved, encouraged, and celebrated failure—so long as the person learned from it. (With her, people got bonus points if they could make others laugh while recounting it.) Sara was also convinced that the only way to achieve big was to risk big. She wanted her staff to act like entrepreneurs: think outside the box and be willing to try new things. The words on her office wall reminded everyone who saw them: "Don't be afraid to fail."[22]

While day-to-day operations had been Laurie Ann's responsibility since 2002, Sara was a regular fixture in the office—until her move to New York seven years later. At that point, as she spent less time with her team, Sara's influence over the culture of the company would have begun to fade. A company's culture is always created and modeled by its leader. Most days, beginning in 2009, that leader was Laurie Ann. Describing herself as someone who was willing to do whatever it took to achieve her goals with 100 percent accuracy, she modeled that drive and commitment to excellence. Laurie Ann also seemed to expect those qualities in her team. "I always like to ask for the seemingly impossible," she later stated. "It's a love-hate relationship—people hate you when you ask it, but they love you when they achieve it."[23]

Laurie Ann also differed from Sara in her perception of and response to failure. And not by just a little bit. Laurie Ann's personal motto hung in large letters above her office desk: "Success is the only option." This appeared to be the polar opposite of Sara's approach. Ironically, Laurie Ann's attitude might have been cultivated by *her* father, just as Sara's had been by hers. Laurie Ann said of her father that he "set the bar so high that sometimes I couldn't touch it." She detailed his expectations, saying, "He was big on hard work and high achievement and the belief that nothing is impossible if you put in the work to get there."[24] After apparently striving for—and feeling like she couldn't reach—perfection as a child, Laurie Ann once described herself as "the most insecure confident person." But rather than seeing insecurity as a problem, she described it as a benefit, saying, "Insecurity is what drives you, and it's the little engine that says I can do better."[25]

By the middle of 2014, Laurie Ann Goldman had departed. And Sara, the woman who once gleefully pointed out to people that she accidentally wore two different shoes to a sales call, was again a fixture in the Spanx offices. And Jan Singer, her newly appointed CEO, brought with her years of industry experience.

## ■ LESSON WE CAN LEARN FROM THE SPANX STORY: INSTILL YOUR VALUES INTO YOUR BUSINESS

If you're creating a business or leading a team, hold fast to your values. "When I first started Spanx," Sara explained, "I was at a cocktail party. A bunch of people had heard I had invented something and came up to me and said, 'You know, Sara, business is war.' I just didn't accept that, and I didn't believe that. I believed that it could be different. I've been focused on the customer, focused on delighting and surprising her, and making her life better, and haven't had any kind of a cutthroat attitude, such as 'other people have to be destroyed or demolished for me to succeed.' That was not my path."[26] Don't ever try to change who you are or compromise your values to be successful.

Jan Singer arrived at Spanx after ten years in various senior leadership roles at Nike, and she immediately got busy assessing the status of Spanx systems, processes, and margins. Capitalizing on the growing popularity of leggings as street style, she responded positively to new ideas from the design team for making Spanx's leggings the best ones out there. She also focused on women's desire to be more comfortable in Spanx products. In 2015, after nearly a year as CEO, she told the *New York Times* what she had noticed about product offerings soon after her arrival at Spanx. She said, "We kept offering reduction," but the company kept hearing stories from women so fed up with hours of discomfort in constricting shapewear that they were "coming home at midnight on Saturday and throwing their Spanx out in the garbage."[27]

Under Jan's leadership, Spanx began moving again in the right direction. And although her tenure was short-lived, during her first year as CEO, the company's revenue shot up from $250 million to $400 million. Jan's positive contributions continued through 2015, as Sara went through a third pregnancy, this time welcoming a daughter, Tepper. But only months after Tepper's birth, Sara made a surprising decision: in 2016, the separate CEO era at Spanx came to an end. Jan departed then, and Sara took over the role of CEO herself. She had come full circle. It was the first time she had taken the lead role since the company moved out of her shared apartment in 2002.

Over the next two years with Sara at the helm, Spanx maintained the positive trajectory, continuing to make changes and improve. The company got slightly leaner, going from 200 employees in 2014 to 194 in 2015, then 189 in 2016. With some restructuring, workloads became more manageable, and efficiency and accountability increased. They also began to advertise more traditionally for the first time ever. And Sara infused her own leadership DNA into Spanx again, strengthening the culture she believed in.

In 2016, Sara brought her personal charm and influence to a new platform. Having avoided all social media for years, she joined Instagram. Immediately, she was able to connect one-on-one with people around the world. Instagram seemed to be the perfect medium for Sara, and she used it to encourage, inspire, and relate to her "tribe." Committed to being herself, she shared everything from professional "oops" moments to makeup-free carpool drop-offs (sometimes with mismatched shoes).

Sara also got back to work on new and risky products. In 2017, Spanx introduced Arm Tights. People laughed initially, skeptical of anyone's need for a kind of long-sleeved crop top made of hosiery, but Sara applied her sales expertise and shared the benefits of Arm Tights when worn under sleeveless tops or dresses, saying they could completely change a look with a pop of color. Many shoppers recognized the value of a lightweight layer under clothes they already owned. Besides changing the look of the dress or shirt they were under, they also added warmth in winter—and even in summer, for those engaged in thermostat battles in air-conditioned offices.

Sara never stopped risking and failing and learning and growing. She sought and found lessons in every experience, then shared them with her staff and followers. When writer Liz Brody asked Sara about the biggest lessons she had ever learned for the December 2018 issue of *Entrepreneur*, Sara responded instantly: learning to fire faster, staying in her lane, and getting better at delegating.[28]

## LESSON WE CAN LEARN FROM THE SPANX STORY: A GREAT PRODUCT SPEAKS TO PEOPLE

After a long run of successes, a need for change might have been hard to see at Spanx. In their first ten years, nearly every effort had resulted in success. But doing what you've always done eventually fails to give you

> what you need to take the next steps in business. Spanx
> only began growing again after some changes occurred.
> What questions do you need to think about asking now
> to be ready for the changes coming tomorrow?

## The Future of Spanx, as One Piece of Sara Blakely's Bigger Picture

As of this writing, the fate of Spanx, and the entire category that the company single-handedly launched, remains to be seen. The company has maintained its success, continuing to report annual earnings around $400 million. Many women still love their Spanx and enthusiastically recommend them to their friends. Hollywood stars are still double-Spanxing and cheerfully admitting it on the red carpet. But as the body positivity movement grows, more people now view Spanx as a symbol of our country's obsession with thinness and "perfection." A growing number are telling the world that they no longer wear shapewear, because they prefer to embrace their beautifully imperfect bodies and let them shine naturally, even if they're not perfectly smooth.

What will happen next at Spanx? Will they continue to grow as a sustainable company for the long term? Or has their product already peaked, with shapewear going the way of the corset, and taking Spanx with it? It's still too early to tell. But if women eventually do stop buying shapewear, Sara can be expected to keep thinking recreationally, asking "why" about everything she observes, and trying to come up with her next big idea.

While the future of Sara's big idea may not be clear, what has been consistent is the reason behind it. From the beginning of her entrepreneurial career, Sara made it her goal to help women. She has said repeatedly that this is the "why" behind her efforts at Spanx. However, the business has never been her only—or even the most important—means to that end.

For over a decade, Sara has poured her resources and influence into her nonprofit organization, which has empowered and equipped women and girls around the world, and continues to do so. That is the final—and most important—chapter of the Spanx story.

"Success cannot be measured in wealth, fame, or power, but by whether you have made a positive difference for others."

—RICHARD BRANSON,
Entrepreneur and Founder of The Virgin Group

portion of the company's earnings to giving away. Surprisingly, after the first profitable full year, the company paid taxes and wasn't paying out to reinvest.

**CHAPTER EIGHT**

# ELEVATING WOMEN

"**T**alk about putting my butt on the line!" This is the story Sara Blakely often tells about that time she convinced the Neiman Marcus buyer to gaze at her posterior in the women's restroom. Since that day, Sara kept "putting her butt on the line," as she convinced the world that they needed what she had to offer.

Spanx may be Sara Blakely, but there is much more to Sara Blakely than Spanx. Selling millions of packages of her products and attaining a net worth of a billion dollars had never been her primary goal. Instead, before she ever invented her first product, she had been dreaming since childhood about doing something that could help women. When the idea for Spanx came along and then the company made it big, the success offered *one* way for her dream of helping women to come true. But it didn't remain the *only* way.

Sara often said the most important purpose of Spanx was always as a platform for giving back. Early on, she set aside a portion of the company's earnings to give away, starting right after the first profits rolled in. "As the company grew," she said, "so did my opportunity to empower women."[1]

## Building a Bigger Platform

One mild Atlanta evening in October of 2006, Sara stood on a banquet hall stage, smiling at hundreds of people. Next to her was her cohost and friend, Sir Richard Branson. They were there to welcome everyone to the first ever "Give a Damn Party." Only two years earlier, Sara had been introduced to the billionaire business mogul before the taping of the first episode of his 2004 reality show, *The Rebel Billionaire*. Even though she had signed on to be a contestant, at the time, Sara's motivation wasn't to compete, much less win money, she said. Instead, involvement in the show was never the end goal. In fact, she said, "I was really interested in learning how to set up a foundation."[2] On set with Richard Branson, she picked his brain about his nonprofit organization, and maybe get his advice on starting hers.

As already mentioned, Sara surprised everyone in the production, especially herself, by avoiding elimination over and over again. In the end, while she made it all the way to the finale, the other contestant won. But just after the winner received his prize money, Richard Branson beckoned her over. In his hand, he held a personal check for $750,000—the amount Fox had paid him to host the show.[3] He handed it to Sara, but it wasn't made out to her, at least not exactly. It was made out to The Sara Blakely Foundation, an organization that did not yet exist. Richard said it was his honor to give the first donation to help Sara establish her foundation. Over the next two years, the foundation was officially created and registered as a nonprofit.

The "Give a Damn Party" in 2006 was the foundation's official launch event. Before the evening was over, $600,000 was raised. And a few months later, The Sara Blakely Foundation began "Empowering Women to Make the World a Better Place," when Sara presented their first charitable gift—the entire $600,000 raised at the event—to a college program in South Africa. It would provide scholarships to 278 young women who would have been otherwise unable to attend college.[4] It appeared that Sara's dream of helping women in other, more significant, ways was coming true.

The Sara Blakely Foundation began "Empowering Women to Make the World a Better Place," when Sara presented their first charitable gift—the entire $600,000 raised at the event—to a college program in South Africa. It would provide scholarships to 278 young women who would have been otherwise unable to attend college.

Explaining her passion for female empowerment, Sara said, "We've been on the planet for a long time, and women have only recently been given the opportunities we so deserve."[5] Comparing her mother's and grandmother's limited choices when they were her age with her own endless options, she said her response was intense gratitude, which she felt compelled to act upon. "Courage comes from the gratitude," she explained. "I'm afraid of most things, but I'll be damned if I wasn't going to try on behalf of all those women who came before me that didn't get the chance."[6]

## Just Getting Started

There is no doubt that Sara had worked hard to get where she was, but she would not take credit for everything she'd accomplished, saying, "I didn't have a lot to do with where I was born."[7] In addition to the blessing of living in the United States, Sara always said she was grateful for another unearned gift: the exposure she'd received from Oprah Winfrey in 2000 when Spanx was just getting off the ground. She hadn't met Oprah in person then, but in early 2007, Sara finally got the opportunity to travel to Chicago and appear on the show.

Seated across from each other onstage, they chatted about the success of Spanx. The picture that had formed in her mind a decade earlier was finally clear. But before the show ended, Sara did one more thing: she surprised Oprah with a gift of one million dollars from her foundation for the Oprah Winfrey Leadership Academy. It was her way of saying thank you for Oprah's kindness, Sara explained, as the audience cheered and the cameras rolled. "To me, the greatest part of success is what you're able to give back," she told Oprah. "And you're a great teacher of that."[8] The two women embraced with tears in their eyes.

## ▪ LESSON WE CAN LEARN FROM THE SPANX STORY: BE KIND TO OTHERS

One of the things Sara said she admired about Richard Branson in addition to his generosity was his kindness. Explaining how she made kindness her goal, she said, "Along the way, some people liked me; some people didn't. As long as I'm in check with my 'why' and my purpose, and I know that I have a good intention and I'm being kind, I've got to let go of all of that other worry."[9] Don't allow distractions or difficulties to keep you from showing consideration and kindness to others.

Sara was invited into a small but elite group in 2013. That summer, she signed The Giving Pledge,[10] joining her friend Richard Branson, as well as other billionaires like Bill and Melinda Gates and Warren Buffett, in committing to dedicate half of her wealth to philanthropy. Stating she would invest specifically in women, Sara said, "I believe it offers one of the greatest returns on investment."[11] With a net worth still estimated at over a billion dollars, she and her foundation had just promised to pour hundreds of millions of dollars into the lives of millions of women. Unleashed and equipped, these women would have the power to become agents of change in their communities and around the world.

In 2013, an important change was made to the name of the charitable organization. It was renamed The Spanx by Sara Blakely Foundation.[12] With a name that now honored and included every Spanx team member, the foundation continued to contribute to causes both in the US and abroad. At this writing, they have donated more than $25 million, primarily to charities that focus on empowering underserved women and girls. It's still a long way from the half of her fortune that she has committed to give away, but the foundation is finding ways to make an impact every day.

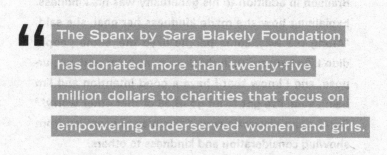

> " The Spanx by Sara Blakely Foundation has donated more than twenty-five million dollars to charities that focus on empowering underserved women and girls.

## What It Means to Be a Female Leader

The types of initiatives and programs the foundation sponsors mirror Sara's creativity. Elevating Women, a program she launched in 2010 as Leg Up, offers mentoring and exposure to dozens of budding female entrepreneurs every year who, according to Melia Patria on ABC News, "have the potential but not the means to grow their businesses."[13] And the Belly Art Project in 2016, which used a fun-loving book filled with colorful images painted on pregnant bellies, along with a massive baby shower for women in need at Atlanta's Grady Hospital,[14] promoted maternal and infant health. The foundation also provides educational opportunities to hundreds of girls who otherwise would not have them, with charities like the Global Village Project, a program for female refugees that encourages careers in the sciences, technology, engineering, and mathematics.[15]

All the programs continue to have one thing in common: elevating women and girls. Sara has described her belief in women's unique approach to leadership, encouraging all women in business to embrace their femininity—and make use of all of its competitive advantages. This can include being dismissed by men. "One of the hardest things about being a woman," Sara explained, "is also one of the greatest: Being underestimated."[16] After all, when a man doesn't view a woman as a worthy competitor, she can often catch him by surprise as she passes him by or shows him up. "Society hasn't equated femininity with power," Sara said. "But I think it's very powerful."[17]

## The Success of Women Doesn't End with the Success of Spanx

Asked in 2016 about how she felt when she first became wealthy, Sara replied, "I loved being able to pay my own rent and stand on my own two feet as a woman. That was a really important thing. But," she continued, "it was really just that I love making the product."[18] Her actions over the years have demonstrated how much she also loved using the wealth earned by the product to make lives better for women.

Sara Blakely is a dreamer—and she nurtured dreams that were much larger than most. But it seems unlikely that even she imagined the heights that she and her company eventually would reach. About her surprise gift to Oprah, she said, "The fact that I was able to write a check for $1 million to something I believe in, it's the American dream."[19] And the joy she felt in giving money was much deeper than any enjoyment felt from earning it. Sara said she preferred to hold on loosely to what she had, because she had so much fun giving—to her foundation, family, and friends. As she said about money, "I think it's fun to make, fun to spend and fun to give away."[20]

# ENDNOTES

## Chapter 1

1. Katherine Schwarzenegger, *I Just Graduated . . . Now What?* (New York: Crown Archetype, 2014), 58.
2. Katherine Schwarzenegger, *I Just Graduated*, 58.
3. Katherine Schwarzenegger, *I Just Graduated*, 59.
4. Jane Mulkerrins, "All Spanx to Sara: Meet Sara Blakely, the woman we have to thank for trimming our tums and boosting our bottoms," *Daily Mail*, April 6, 2013, https://www.dailymail .co.uk/home/you/article-2303499/Meet-Spanx-creator-Sarah -Blakely.html.
5. Sara Blakely, "How Spanx Got Started," filmed December 1, 2011, at the Inc. Women's Summit, New York, *Inc.*, January 12, 2012, video and transcript, 13:34, https://www.inc.com/sara -blakely/how-sara-blakley-started-spanx.html.
6. Luisa Kroll, "Forbes World's Billionaires 2012," *Forbes*, March 7, 2012, https://www.forbes.com/sites/luisakroll/2012/03/07 /forbes-worlds-billionaires-2012/#5cb0343c2c9d.

## Chapter 2

1. Katherine Schwarzenegger, *I Just Graduated*, 53.
2. Candice Dyer, "The Joy of Spanx," *Atlanta* magazine, June 1, 2004, https://www.atlantamagazine.com/great-reads/spanx/.
3. Juju Chang and Melia Patria, "Spanx, Re-Shaping Women's Self-Confidence, Opens Stores," ABC News, November 29, 2012, https://abcnews.go.com/Business/spanx-shaping-womens -confidence-opens-stores/story?id=17815019#.ULkEjKpbaw5.
4. Candice Dyer, "The Joy of Spanx."

5. Candice Dyer, "The Joy of Spanx."

6. Clare O'Connor, "American Booty," *Forbes*, March 26, 2012, appeared online as "How Sara Blakely of Spanx Turned $5,000 into $1 billion," *Forbes*, March 14, 2012, https://www.forbes.com /global/2012/0326/billionaires-12-feature-united-states-spanx -sara-blakely-american-booty.html#1ab317b17ea0.

7. Jane Mulkerrins, "All Spanx to Sara."

8. Jill Becker, "Shaping Sara Blakely: Meet the Billionaire Founder of Spanx," *Success*, January 2016, posted December 7, 2015, https://www.success.com/shaping-sara-blakely-meet-the -billionaire-founder-of-spanx/.

9. Louise France, "The Woman in Control of America's Bottom," *Guardian*, April 13, 2008, https://www.theguardian.com /lifeandstyle/2008/apr/13/women.fashion2.

10. Louise France, "The Woman in Control of America's Bottom."

11. Clare O'Connor, "American Booty."

12. Louise France, "The Woman in Control of America's Bottom," *Guardian*, April 13, 2008, https://www.theguardian.com /lifeandstyle/2008/apr/13/women.fashion2.

13. Katherine Schwarzenegger, *I Just Graduated*, 57.

14. Katherine Schwarzenegger, *I Just Graduated*, 57.

15. Jill Becker, "Shaping Sara Blakely."

16. Wes Moss, *Starting from Scratch: Secrets from 21 Ordinary People Who Made the Entrepreneurial Leap* (Chicago: Dearborn Trade Publishing, 2005), 65.

17. Clare O'Connor, "American Booty."

18. Clare O'Connor, "American Booty."

19. Gillian Zoe Segal, *Getting There: A Book of Mentors*, (New York: Harry N. Abrams, 2015), 33.

20. Gillian Zoe Segal, *Getting There*, 33.

21. Gillian Zoe Segal, *Getting There*, 33.

22. Gillian Zoe Segal, *Getting There*, 33.

23. Susie Moore, "What Interviewing Sara Blakely Taught Me," Susie -Moore.com, accessed January 24, 2019, https://susie-moore .com/interview/sara-blakely-interview (date unknown).

24. Susie Moore, "What Interviewing Sara Blakely Taught Me."

25. Katherine Schwarzenegger, *I Just Graduated*, 54.

26. Robert Frank, "Billionaire Sara Blakely Says the Secret to Success Is Failure," CNBC, October 16, 2013, https://www.cnbc

.com/2013/10/16/billionaire-sara-blakely-says-secret-to-success
-is-failure.html.

27. Katherine Schwarzenegger, *I Just Graduated*, 55.
28. Clare O'Connor, "American Booty."
29. Gillian Zoe Segal, *Getting There*, 34.
30. Gillian Zoe Segal, *Getting There*, 34.
31. Clare O'Connor, "American Booty."
32. Clare O'Connor, "American Booty."
33. Gillian Zoe Segal, *Getting There*, 34.
34. Gillian Zoe Segal, *Getting There*, 34.
35. Liz Brody, "Spanx Founder Sara Blakely Has 99 Pages of Business Ideas," *Entrepreneur*, December, 2018, posted November 28, 2018, https://www.entrepreneur.com/article/322936.
36. Jane Mulkerrins, "All Spanx to Sara."
37. Katherine Schwarzenegger, *I Just Graduated*, 56.
38. Katherine Schwarzenegger, *I Just Graduated*, 56.
39. Danielle Weiner-Bronner, "She Was too Short to Play Goofy. Then She Invented Spanx. Now She's a Billionaire," CNN Business, April 2, 2018, https://money.cnn.com/2018/04/02/news/companies/sara-blakely-rebound/index.html.
40. Jill Becker, "Shaping Sara Blakely."
41. Jill Becker, "Shaping Sara Blakely."
42. Gillian Zoe Segal, *Getting There*, 34.
43. Wes Moss, *Starting from Scratch*, 65.
44. Wes Moss, *Starting from Scratch*, 71–72.
45. Reid Hoffman and Sara Blakely, "How to Find Your Big Idea," *Masters of Scale* Podcast, Episode 22, audio and transcript, 41:00, March 20, 2018, https://mastersofscale.com/sara-blakely-how-to-find-your-big-idea/.
46. Jill Becker, "Shaping Sara Blakely."
47. Reid Hoffman and Sara Blakely, "How to Find Your Big Idea."
48. Juju Chang and Melia Patria, "Re-Shaping Women's Self-Confidence."
49. Wes Moss, *Starting from Scratch*, 66.

## Chapter 3

1. Sara Blakely, "How Spanx Got Started."
2. Clare O'Connor, "American Booty."

3. Blaire Briody, "Sara Blakely: Start Small, Think Big, Scale Fast," Insights by Stanford Business, June 21, 2018, https://www.gsb .stanford.edu/insights/sara-blakely-start-small-think-big-scale -fast.

4. Gillian Zoe Segal, *Getting There*, 34.

5. Jill Becker, "Shaping Sara Blakely."

6. Jill Becker, "Shaping Sara Blakely."

7. Jill Becker, "Shaping Sara Blakely."

8. Gillian Zoe Segal, *Getting There*, 34–35.

9. Sara Blakely, "How Spanx Got Started."

10. Sara Blakely, "How Spanx Got Started."

11. Sara Blakely (@sarablakely), Instagram video caption, December 17, 2018, https://www.instagram.com/p/BrfYA3kAXHD/.

12. Sara Blakely, interview with Guy Raz, "How a Pitch in a Neiman Marcus Ladies Room Changed Sara Blakely's Life," How I Built This on NPR, audio interview and transcript, September 12, 2016, https://www.npr.org/templates/transcript/transcript.php ?storyId=493312213.

13. Sara Blakely, "How Spanx Got Started."

14. Wes Moss, *Starting from Scratch*, 66.

15. Ieva M. Augstums, "Sheer Hosiery Sales Continue to Slip," *Los Angeles Times*, December 26, 2006, http://articles.latimes.com /2006/dec/26/business/fi-pantyhose26.

16. Troy Patterson, "The Politics of Pantyhose," *New York Times Magazine*, October 4, 2015, https://www.nytimes.com/2015/10/04 /magazine/the-politics-of-pantyhose.html.

17. Wes Moss, *Starting from Scratch*, 66.

18. Wes Moss, *Starting from Scratch*, 66.

19. Wes Moss, *Starting from Scratch*, 67.

20. Wes Moss, *Starting from Scratch*, 67.

21. Leigh Gallagher, "Footless and Fancy-Free," *Forbes*, April 2, 2001, https://www.forbes.com/forbes/2001/0402/120.html#c243 c0945620.

22. Sara Blakely, "How Spanx Got Started."

23. Sara Blakely, "How Spanx Got Started."

24. Sara Blakely, "How Spanx Got Started."

25. "Size Chart," L'eggs Sheer Energy Control Top, Sheer Toe Pantyhose 6-pack, Hanes, accessed January 23, 2019, https://www

.onehanesplace.com/shop/onehanesplace/leggs-sheer-energy
-pantyhose-65410.

26. Sara Blakely, "How Spanx Got Started."
27. Sara Blakely, "How Spanx Got Started."
28. Gabrielle Karol, "How Sara Blakely Built a Billion-Dollar Business from Scratch," Fox Business, October 22, 2014, https://www.foxbusiness.com/features/sara-blakely-how-she-built-a-billion-dollar-business-from-scratch.
29. Robert Frank, "Billionaire Sara Blakely Says the Secret to Success Is Failure," CNBC, October 16, 2013, https://www.cnbc.com/2013/10/16/billionaire-sara-blakely-says-secret-to-success-is-failure.html.
30. Sara Blakely and Guy Raz, "Pitch."
31. *Masters of Scale* (transcript).
32. Sara Blakely, "How Spanx Got Started."
33. Sara Blakely, "How Spanx Got Started."
34. Sara Blakely, "How Spanx Got Started."
35. Jane Mulkerrins, "All Spanx to Sara."
36. Jane Mulkerrins, "All Spanx to Sara."
37. Sara Blakely and Guy Raz, "Pitch."

## Chapter 4

1. Bruce Horovitz, "Women Will Model Bras in TV Ads as Decades-Old Taboo Falls," *Los Angeles Times*, April 21, 1987, http://articles.latimes.com/1987-04-21/business/fi-341_1_tv-ads.
2. Sara Blakely, "How Spanx Got Started."
3. Sara Blakely, "How Spanx Got Started."
4. Sara Blakely, "How Spanx Got Started."
5. Clare O'Connor, "American Booty."
6. Sara Blakely, "How Spanx Got Started."
7. Wes Moss, *Starting from Scratch*, 69.
8. Wes Moss, *Starting from Scratch*, 69.
9. Alexandra Jacobs, "Smooth Moves: How Sara Blakely Rehabilitated the Girdle," *New Yorker*, March 28, 2011, https://www.newyorker.com/magazine/2011/03/28/smooth-moves.
10. Sara Blakely and Guy Raz, "Pitch."
11. Sara Blakely and Guy Raz, "Pitch."

12. Louise France, "The Woman in Control."
13. Louise France, "The Woman in Control."
14. Susie Moore, "What Sara Blakely Wished She Knew in Her 20s," *Marie Claire*, November 4, 2014, https://www.marieclaire.com /politics/news/a11508/sara-blakely-interview/.
15. Sara Blakely and Guy Raz, "Pitch."
16. Sara Blakely and Guy Raz, "Pitch."
17. Sara Blakely and Guy Raz, "Pitch."
18. Wes Moss, *Starting from Scratch*, 70.
19. Helen Lock, "'I Put My Butt on the Line': How Spanx Took Over the World," *Guardian*, July 11, 2016, https://www.theguardian .com/small-business-network/2016/jul/11/put-butt-on-the -line-how-spanx-world.
20. Jill Becker, "21 Bits of Wit and Wisdom from the Woman behind the Billion-Dollar Brand," *Success*, December 8, 2015, accessed January 31, 2019, https://www.success.com/21-bits-of-wit-and -wisdom-from-the-woman-behind-the-billion-dollar-brand/.
21. Blaire Briody, "Start Small."
22. Sara Blakely, interview by Randi Zuckerberg, "Leading Ladies with Sara Blakely," SiriusXM Stars and Business Radio, audio, 1:58, June 28, 2017, https://soundcloud.com/siriusxmentertainment /when-sara-blakely-store-section.
23. Sara Blakely, "Leading Ladies with Sara Blakely."
24. Blaire Briody, "Start Small."
25. Wes Moss, *Starting from Scratch*, 70.
26. Jill Becker, "Shaping Sara Blakely."
27. Clare O'Connor, "Top Five Startup Tips from Spanx Billionaire Sara Blakely," *Forbes*, April 2, 2012, https://www.forbes.com /sites/clareoconnor/2012/04/02/top-five-startup-tips-from -spanx-billionaire-sara-blakely/#1c5f246319b4.
28. Jill Becker, "Shaping Sara Blakely."

## Chapter 5

1. Jack Neff, "How to Get Your Brand on 'Oprah,'" *Ad Age*, June 2, 2008, https://adage.com/article/madisonvine-news/brand -oprah/127457/.
2. Joyce Millman, "The Road to the White House Goes through Oprah," *Salon*, September 25, 2000, https://www.salon.com /2000/09/25/oprah_10/.

3. Clay Halton, "Oprah Effect," Investopedia, Updated April 23, 2018, https://www.investopedia.com/terms/o/oprah-effect.asp.

4. Wes Moss, *Starting from Scratch*, 70.

5. Sara Blakely, "Differentiating Her Business Idea," filmed December 1, 2011, at the Inc. Women's Summit, New York, *Inc.*, video and transcript, 5:35, January 20, 2012, https://www.inc.com/sara-blakely/how-sara-blakely-differentiated-her-business-idea-for-spanx.html.

6. Reid Hoffman and Sara Blakely, "How to Find Your Big Idea."

7. Sara Blakely, "Differentiating Her Business Idea."

8. Louise France, "The Woman in Control."

9. Jill Becker, "Shaping Sara Blakely."

10. Clare O'Connor, "American Booty."

11. Sara Blakely (@sarablakely), "#Tbt 2000. I was sitting in my apartment 'aka' my headquarters with no money to advertise, and I got the call that @oprah chose spanx as her favorite product of the year!!!" Facebook video, November 2, 2017, https://www.facebook.com/sarablakely/videos/482108915504900/.

12. Thomson Gale, "Spanx, Inc," *International Directory of Company Histories*, 2006, Online at Encyclopedia.com, accessed February 2, 2019, https://www.encyclopedia.com/books/politics-and-business-magazines/spanx-inc.

13. Leigh Gallagher, "Footless and Fancy-Free."

14. Clare O'Connor, "How Spanx Became a Billion-Dollar Business without Advertising," *Forbes* online, March 12, 2012, https://www.forbes.com/sites/clareoconnor/2012/03/12/how-spanx-became-a-billion-dollar-business-without-advertising/#7b633744d646.

15. Gillian Zoe Segal, *Getting There*, 36.

## Chapter 6

1. Jill Becker, "Shaping Sara Blakely."

2. Alexandra Kaptik, "How Do You Get Your Product on a TV Shopping Network?" *Wall Street Journal Online*, March 17, 2003, https://www.wsj.com/articles/SB104749893124232500.

3. Thomson Gale, "Spanx, Inc," *International Directory of Company Histories*, 2006, Online at Encyclopedia.com, accessed February 2, 2019, https://www.encyclopedia.com/books/politics-and-business-magazines/spanx-inc.

4. Richard Feloni, "'Shark Tank' investor Lori Greiner explains why she still invests in 'one-hit wonder' companies," *Business Insider*, April 27, 2015, https://www.businessinsider.com/shark -tanks-lori-greiner-on-how-she-invests-in-products-2015-4.

5. Richard Feloni, "'Shark Tank' investor Lori Greiner."

6. Richard Feloni, "'Shark Tank' investor Lori Greiner."

7. Blaire Briody, "Start Small."

8. Spanx, "About Us," accessed February 2, 2019, https://www .spanx.com/about-us.

9. Blaire Briody, "Start Small."

10. Sara Blakely, "Sara Blakely and the Skinny on Spanx," *Forbes* Under 30 Boston Summit, video 17:50, filmed October 19, 2018, https://www.forbes.com/video/5850945408001/#69c25096f3cd.

11. Wes Moss, *Starting from Scratch*, 71.

12. Sara Blakely and Guy Raz, "Pitch."

13. Alexandra Kaptik, "Get Your Product on a TV Shopping Network."

14. Alexandra Kaptik, "Get Your Product on a TV Shopping Network."

15. Alexandra Kaptik, "Get Your Product on a TV Shopping Network."

16. Thomson Gale, "Spanx, Inc."

17. Thomson Gale, "Spanx, Inc."

18. Candice Dyer, "The Joy of Spanx."

19. Clare O'Connor, "Top Five Startup Tips from Spanx Billionaire Sara Blakely," *Forbes*, April 2, 2012, https://www.forbes.com /sites/clareoconnor/2012/04/02/top-five-startup-tips-from -spanx-billionaire-sara-blakely/#1c5f246319b4.

20. Colleen Leahey, "SPANX CEO Out after Building the Mega- brand," *Fortune*, February 11, 2014, accessed February 19, 2019, http://fortune.com/2014/02/11/spanx-ceo-out-after-building -the-mega-brand/.

21. Colleen Leahey, "SPANX CEO."

22. Colleen Leahey, "SPANX CEO."

23. Clare O'Connor, "Top Five Startup Tips."

24. Colleen Leahey, "SPANX CEO."

25. Marcia Heroux Pounds, "Don't Fear Failure Entrepreneur Says," *South Florida Sun Sentinel*, March 27, 2006, https://www .sun-sentinel.com/news/fl-xpm-2006-03-27-0603240466-story .html.

26. Spanx company timeline, http://press.spanx.com/_ir/117/20131 /Vertical%20Timeline_16x10_2.6.pdf, Downloaded 2/23/19.

27.  Jane Mulkerrins, "All Spanx to Sara."
28.  Thomson Gale, "Spanx, Inc."
29.  Candice Dyer, "The Joy of Spanx."
30.  Candice Dyer, "The Joy of Spanx."
31.  Jane Mulkerrins, "All Spanx to Sara."
32.  Susie Moore, "Interviewing Sara Blakely."
33.  Stephanie Thompson, "Spanx," *Ad Age*, November 7, 2005, https://adage.com/article/special-report-marketing-50/spanx/105139/.
34.  Stephanie Thompson, "Spanx."
35.  Louise France, "The Woman in Control."
36.  "Spanx Press Kit," Spanx.com, 2012, http://press.spanx.com/_ir/117/20125/2012_Spanx_Press_Kit.pdf, Downloaded 1/1/19.
37.  Alison Fass, "Hip Girdles," *Forbes*, September 29, 2006, https://www.forbes.com/forbes/2006/1016/046b.html#5f75ce816cab.
38.  Candice Dyer, "The Joy of Spanx."
39.  "For those with something to hide," *Mercury News*, February 24, 2007, https://www.mercurynews.com/2007/02/24/for-those-with-something-to-hide/.
40.  Clare O'Connor, "American Booty."
41.  Candice Dyer, "The Joy of Spanx."
42.  Stephanie Thompson, "Spanx."
43.  Meredith Bryan, "Spanx Me, Baby!" *Observer*, December 5, 2007, https://observer.com/2007/12/spanx-me-baby/.
44.  Betsy Kroll, "Sara Blakely: Body-Shaper Pioneer," *Time*, September 9, 2009, http://content.time.com/time/specials/packages/article/0,28804,1921163_1921155_1921161,00.html.
45.  Meredith Bryan, "Spanx Me, Baby!"
46.  Meredith Bryan, "Spanx Me, Baby!"
47.  Emily Cronin, "Thanks, Mrs Spanx! Meet billionaire underwear guru Sara Blakely," *Telegraph*, July 24, 2016, https://www.telegraph.co.uk/fashion/people/thanks-mrs-spanx-meet-billionaire-underwear-guru-sara-blakely/.

## Chapter 7

1.  Clare O'Connor, "American Booty."
2.  Zoe Wood, "Sara Blakely: a woman with a great grasp of figures," *Guardian*, March 10, 2012, https://www.theguardian.com

/theobserver/2012/mar/11/observer-profile-sara-blakely
-spanx.

3. Clare O'Connor, "American Booty."

4. Clare O'Connor, "Top Five Startup Tips."

5. Clare O'Connor, "American Booty."

6. Betsy Kroll, "Body-Shaper Pioneer."

7. Betsy Kroll, "Body-Shaper Pioneer."

8. Mark Gordon, "Make It Happen," *Business Observer FL*, April 25, 2014, https://www.businessobserverfl.com/article/make-it
-happen.

9. Juju Chang and Melia Patria, "Re-Shaping Women's Self-Confidence."

10. Sara Blakely and Jesse Itzler, "Advice from Married Entrepreneurs Sara Blakely and Jesse Itzler," interviewed by Elizabeth Atwater, Babson Thought and Action, Babson College, November 21, 2018, http://entrepreneurship.babson.edu/married
-entrepreneurs-advice/.

11. Zoe Wood, "Sara Blakely."

12. "Timeline on the Great Recession," *Christian Science Monitor*, September 8, 2013, https://www.csmonitor.com/Business/2013
/0908/Timeline-on-the-Great-Recession.

13. "Lip Service," *Economist*, January 23, 2009, https://www
.economist.com/unknown/2009/01/23/lip-service.

14. Cheryl Tan, "Lunchtime Snap: The New Hosiery Index? Sales Crept Up as Economy Went Down," *Wall Street Journal*, November 10, 2008, https://blogs.wsj.com/runway/2008/11/10
/lunchtime-snap-the-hosiery-index-sales-crept-up-as-economy
-went-down/.

15. Alexandra Jacobs, "Smooth Moves."

16. Candice Dyer, "The Joy of Spanx."

17. Alexandra Jacobs, "Smooth Moves."

18. Alexandra Jacobs, "Smooth Moves."

19. Liza Graves, "FACES of the South: Laurie Ann Goldman, CEO of Spanx," *Style Blueprint* (date unclear, but between late 2013 and her departure in February 2014), accessed February 27, 2019, https://styleblueprint.com/nashville/everyday/sb-faces
-of-the-south-laurie-ann-goldman-ceo-of-spanx/.

20. Jennifer Larino, "8 Lessons Former Spanx CEO Learned While Leading a Hosiery Revolution," *New Orleans Times-Picayune*, September 9, 2014, accessed February 27, 2019, https://www.nola.com/business/2014/09/8_things_the_former_spanx_ceo_1.html.

21. Carla Caldwell, "Spanx CEO steps down," *Atlanta Business Journal*, February 13, 2014, https://www.bizjournals.com/atlanta/morning_call/2014/02/spanx-ceo-goldman-steps-down-high.html?page=all.

22. Alexandra Jacobs, "Smooth Moves."

23. Laura Emily Dunn, "Women in Business: Laurie Ann Goldman, Leading Retailing Executive," *HuffPost*, October 13, 2014, https://www.huffingtonpost.com/laura-dunn/women-in-business-laurie_b_5977152.html.

24. Laura Emily Dunn, "Women in Business."

25. Laura Emily Dunn, "Women in Business."

26. Ina Paiva Cordle, "Former Spanx CEO's Career Advice: Be Yourself," *Miami Herald*, October 23, 2014, https://www.miamiherald.com/news/business/article3335031.html.

27. Hiroko Tabuchi, "Behind the Curve: Spanx Tries to Loosen Up Its Image," *New York Times*, April 25, 2015, https://www.nytimes.com/2015/04/25/business/spanx-tries-to-loosen-up-its-image.html.

28. Liz Brody, "99 Pages of Business Ideas."

## Chapter 8

1. "About," The Spanx Foundation, accessed March 7, 2019, http://www.spanxfoundation.com/about/.

2. "About."

3. "About."

4. "Our Journey," The Spanx Foundation, accessed March 7, 2019, http://www.spanxfoundation.com/journey/.

5. Sara Blakely, "Today is Nannie's Birthday," Instagram photo, February 5, 2019, accessed March 3, 2019, https://www.instagram.com/p/BthcsmiALVm/.

6. Sara Blakely, "Today is Nannie's Birthday."

7. Juju Chang and Melia Patria, "Re-Shaping Women's Self-Confidence."

8. "How'd They Do That," *The Oprah Winfrey Show*, February 1, 2007, Episode Summary at Oprah.com, http://www.oprah.com /oprahshow/howd-they-do-that.

9. Susie Moore, "What Sara Blakely Wished She Knew."

10. Sara Blakely, "My Giving Pledge," The Giving Pledge, accessed March 8, 2019, https://givingpledge.org/Pledger.aspx?id=169.

11. Jenna Goudreau, "Billionaire Sara Blakely Pledges to Give Away Half of Her Fortune," *Entrepreneur*, May 8, 2013, https://www .entrepreneur.com/article/226601.

12. Based on federal filings on CharityNavigator.com, accessed March 8, 2019.

13. Melia Patria, "Spanx Founder Reveals How to Build a Billion-Dollar Business," ABC News, November 29, 2012, https:// abcnews.go.com/Business/build-billion-dollar-business-spanx -inventor-sara-blakely/story?id=17831265.

14. "Our Journey."

15. "Our Journey."

16. Mary Logan Bikoff, "The Uplifter: How Spanx CEO Sara Blakely Became One of the Most Inspirational Women in Business," *Atlanta* magazine, December 2017, https://www.atlantamagazine .com/style/uplifter-how-spanx-ceo-sara-blakely-became-one -of-the-most-inspirational-women-in-business/.

17. Mary Logan Bikoff, "The Uplifter."

18. Sara Blakely and Guy Raz, "Pitch."

19. Chary Southmayd, "Hometown Girl Makes American Dream Come True," *Tampa Bay Newspapers—Belle Aire Bee*, February 7, 2007, https://www.tbnweekly.com/belleair_bee/article_3abb 0e86-540b-5cb6-9fc7-b2dc00cd99c1.html.

20. Emily Cronin, "Thanks, Mrs Spanx!"

# INDEX

# THE
# TARGET
# STORY

Available now from HarperCollins Leadership

# FOUNDING STORY

arget's brand promise is simple, yet complex: "Expect more. Pay less."

Fulfilling that idealistic promise requires expertise in areas like supply chain, inventory control, replenishment, merchandising, marketing, customer service, advertising, and innovation to name a few. Putting all those pieces together, working as one, has enabled the retail giant to "help all families discover the joy of everyday life." Satisfying "guests" is the secret sauce that has fueled Target's immense success.

Today, Target has over 350,000 employees and operates stores in all fifty states and in the District of Columbia. Approximately 75 percent of the US population lives within ten miles of a Target store, giving them easy accessibility. The company is a talent-based organization that is heavily immersed in its culture and core values. Those values and the culture have evolved to reflect a more modern-day retail organization, yet the purpose of helping all families discover joy is grounded in the chain's foundation.

"I think that there are some principles that have been long lasting in the company," said Brian Cornell, Target CEO and chairman. "The focus on giving back. . . . And this general belief that if we're doing the right things for our communities, and making communities stronger, our business will also benefit. But I think that goes all the way back to the founding family."

## How It All Began

George Draper Dayton was born on March 6, 1857, in Clifton Springs, New York, in the western part of the state.

The Daytons' family lineage could be traced back to Ralph Dayton, a shoemaker who arrived to the New World in the 1600s from County Kent, England. Ralph eventually settled in East Hampton, New York, where he served as the town's constable as well as an interpreter to the Native Americans. Another relative, Jonathan Dayton, earned recognition as a New Jersey politician and for being the youngest to sign the United States Constitution; Dayton, Ohio, was named after him.

George's parents, David and Caroline Dayton, were a religious couple. David was a successful doctor and surgeon as well as a devout Presbyterian; his wife was a Methodist. Their actions set an altruistic example for George, who gravitated to the church. After passing the entrance exam for Hobart College in 1873, he hoped to enroll and study to become a minister. But his plans changed when the Panic of 1873 thrust the country into a depression.

George had worked at a nursery since the age of eleven, where he made 37½ cents a day. He continued to work at the nursery the summer after finishing high school in Clifton, New York. That fall of 1873, his father took note of how many businesses were already experiencing financial difficulty. George McMillan ran one of the stressed businesses and asked Dr. Dayton for financial help. That led Dr. Dayton to offer an apprenticeship for his son's services. McMillan, who had his hands in a number of businesses, including lumber and coal interests, paid George a salary of $800 per year with a 3 percent commission. George took the job, operating on the belief that he would build a nest egg for himself before following through with his college plans. Though he was only sixteen, George had a work ethic that caught McMillan off guard. He had not fathomed that George would earn any commission. But George's ambition led him to solicit sales in the evenings. George wrote the following about the experience: "I had drawn very little of the salary, so around fifteen hundred dollars were due and Mr. McMillan could not pay. He suggested I buy the coal and lumberyard."

George borrowed money from his father and became owner of the business at seventeen. While his work ethic helped him thrive in his business, the hours he kept eventually took their toll. After trying to work consecutive twenty-four-hour shifts, he got sick, prompting Dr. Dayton to sell his son's business and help him regain his health. When George recovered, he returned to the workplace with perspective. John Mackay, who owned a lumberyard and had a banking business, hired Dayton.

Through investments and the sale of his business, George managed to save $5,000 by age twenty-one, paving the way for him to marry his longtime sweetheart, Emma Chadwick, on December 17, 1878, in Montour Falls, New York.

## George Goes to Minneapolis

Emma's parents were both heavily invested in education. Her father, Edmund C. Chadwick, a professor, had even been a classmate and personal friend of Ralph Waldo Emerson. Emma quite naturally was drawn to her profession as a teacher.

Having experienced the struggles created by a lack of money, George and Emma agreed to set aside $5 every week, putting into place a shared habit of saving.

Among George's duties while working for Mackay were to be in charge of his office and banking business. Typical of George, he had wowed Mackay with his business acumen, as well as New York investors, who were so impressed by George's business mind, judgment, and integrity that they enlisted him to help with their mortgage holdings in the Midwest. They sent George to Worthington, Minnesota, to gain insight into why the investments they'd made through the local bank, the Bank of Worthington, had gone south. George followed instructions, then reported back to the New York investors that Minnesota farmers had suffered a six-year run of bad luck that included a grasshopper scourge and bad weather. The effects of those circumstances had proved devastating, prompting many to leave behind their farms and their debts. George suggested that the investors ought to put somebody in place locally to look after their investments. They agreed and urged George to become that guy. Backed by investors, he bought the Bank of Worthington and moved to Worthington to take charge of the bank in April of 1883.

George sorted out the bank's bad mortgages and debts then resold the land, even convincing the New York investors to put more money into Worthington. That exercise led to his forming the Minnesota Loan & Investment Co. of Worthington, which concentrated on buying and selling farm property and lending money to farmers.

By the 1890s, George and his cohorts at Minnesota Loan & Investment expanded their interests to include city properties. George checked out the prospects for several cities, including Salt Lake City, St. Paul, Omaha, St. Louis, Kansas City, and Minneapolis. Minneapolis served as a railroad hub and boasted of healthy lumber and flour mill industries on the Mississippi River, which influenced George's decision. He never looked back, immersing himself in what would become a lifelong love affair with Minneapolis and its community.

Executing his due diligence as he began his search for prime real estate, George would count people on downtown street corners. "As I was not known by many in the city, I felt free to stand on corners and count the people pass," Dayton said.

Most figured the logical, and best, prospects for downtown real estate would be in close proximity to the flour mills and the Mississippi River. George's research told him otherwise, directing him to concentrate his purchases along Nicollet Avenue, between Fourth and Tenth Streets, or "uptown" as opposed to "downtown." Dayton's strategy proved wise, increasing his wealth while expanding his interests in the evolving Midwestern city.

## The Fire

Fire brought a constant threat to Minneapolis in the late nineteenth century. The area had sustained droughts in 1893 and 1894, which left the city parched and ripe to go up in flames with the slightest spark. On August 13, 1893, the most devastating fire in the city's history occurred, igniting approximately twenty-three city blocks.

By 1895, however, conditions had changed, due in large part to the end of the drought. The total number of alarms sounded dropped 30 percent, and the losses due to fire were reduced by 45 percent. Still, two memorable fires dotted the Minneapolis landscape that year.

A June 27 fire at MacDonald Brothers' crockery warehouse left five firefighters dead, the worst loss of life in the Minneapolis Fire Department's history. Less than three months later, the Westminster Presbyterian Church caught fire in the early morning of September 6, 1895. A general alarm rang out at around 2:30 a.m., sending firefighters to the church's location at the corner of Nicollet Avenue and Seventh Street. The fire had ignited in the roof over the main part of the large church. Getting water to the flames proved to be a logistical nightmare. By the time firefighters had extinguished the fire, the church had been destroyed.

Bystanders from the surrounding neighborhoods had been awakened by the bells and whistles. They watched the fire department's efforts and were astounded when the roof gave way. Critiques of the department followed. Surely, if they had located the fire hoses in a more strategic fashion, the church would not have met its fate.

The fire left the church in a pickle. Rebuilding wasn't in the cards because its insurance failed to cover the cost of the damage. And the prospects for selling were dismal since real estate had tumbled due to a recession. Several Minneapolis business leaders looked to George Dayton to help rectify the church's problem. He came through, buying the distressed property early in 1896 for $165,000.

Allen Hill, the secretary of the Westminster board of trustees, expressed gratitude following the transaction. "I do not know what Mr. Dayton's intentions are with regard to the property, but I do know that we feel relieved that the matter has finally settled. The price we consider but a fair one, and now the church feels at liberty to take immediate steps toward the purchase of a location and the erection of a new church."

Dayton's plans remained unclear, but he continued to purchase property in the proximity of the Westminster lot until he possessed full frontage along Nicollet Avenue between Seventh and Eighth Streets. The Westminster property remained an eyesore, even after Dayton's purchase, prompting Minneapolis building inspector John A. Gilman to notify Dayton that the remaining walls were unsafe and needed to be removed.

Dayton made a deal to sell the property to a group of Chicago investors, who had grandiose plans for the Westminster church site. After a prolonged negotiation, the Chicago investors agreed to buy it for $2,000 per front foot on the 215 feet on Nicollet Avenue, where they planned to build a fireproof, ten-story, European-style hotel. Several details of the agreement needed to be worked out before the deal was finalized, but the Chicago group had enough confidence about the project going forward that they hired an architect to rush plans for the $500,000 hotel. However, when one of the investors visited Minneapolis, he learned that the proposed hotel would be located in a dry zone, meaning the hotel's bar would not be able to serve alcohol. That detail turned into a deal-breaker. The investor wired his partners to tell them what he told Dayton, that the deal was "dead as a door nail."

Finally, Dayton decided to build a six-story building on the Westminster site. The building covered 215 feet on Nicollet Avenue and 140 feet on Seventh Street and would be composed of brick, iron, plate glass, and the "latest patterns" in pressed brick and terra cotta.

Construction began in 1901 and was completed in 1902. Dayton's solution for having a tenant came when he convinced the R.S. Goodfellow Company, Minneapolis's fourth-largest department store, to move into the building. Dayton bought a share of retiring owner Reuben Simon Goodfellow's interest in the store. Believing that Minneapolis's citizens wanted to patronize businesses that were operated by locals, Dayton persuaded several residents to become part of the venture's ownership. J.B. Mosher, a local businessman with a wealth of retail experience, and George London, a longtime Goodfellow's employee, bought the other shares of Good-fellow's interest. Dayton wanted to remain in the background as a silent partner and harbored no aspirations of becoming a merchant.

Along with the change in ownership came a new name, Goodfellow Dry Goods Co. A soft opening took place on June 2, 1902. The formal opening of the store followed twenty-two days later. The new store—referred to as the "Daylight" store—offered virtually anything a shopper might want, from high fashion to practical items. According to the *Minneapolis Journal*'s account of the store's formal opening, "There is plenty of 'elbow' and breathing room, and the store is immaculate from its splendid basement to its sixth floor."

## A New Venture

Corresponding with the store's opening, Dayton moved his family from Worthington to Minneapolis. He and his wife now had four children: Draper, Caroline, Nelson, and Josephine. On July 14, 1902, he sold his house in Worthington, had all of his family's belongings loaded onto a railroad car, and headed to Minneapolis to begin a new adventure in the city.

Despite the grandiose nature of the formal opening, many local businessmen believed that Dayton had missed the mark with his enterprise and that he would lose his shirt. Others had passed on buying the Westminster property due to its location in the uptown area, away from the more popular loop district. But Dayton proved the naysayers wrong when Goodfellow Dry Goods Company doubled its sales in its first year. He then bought out one of his partners, who had shown himself to be shady in his financial dealings; shortly thereafter, he bought out the other partner.

Dayton pressed hard to turn increased sales into profitability, but never strayed from the virtuous path he traveled, which included providing to customers quality, service, and honesty. Finally, in 1906, the store turned the corner, realizing a profit for the first time.

Dayton committed to offering customers a vast variety of options from tools to high-fashion clothes. Dayton even went as far as to send an employee, Theodore Mayer, to Deauville, France, to study French styles in one of the most fashionable cities in the world. Upon his return, purchases from the trip became available in-store, and reproductions of the most beautiful wraps, gowns, and other fashions Mayer saw were made and sold to customers.

Dayton's made sure its shelves were always fully stocked with merchandise, and the store would go to great lengths to ensure that nothing interfered with fulfilling this goal. In 1920, the railroad executed a freight embargo, which interfered with Dayton's ability to receive shipments. Demonstrating just how far the store would go to prevent shortages, Dayton's hired two airplanes to send eight hundred pounds of freight from New

York to Minneapolis. It was the longest cargo-carrying flight ever made for commercial purposes.

Dayton converted the basement floor to an area where customers could shop for items at lower prices. The assortment of less expensive merchandise included apparel for men, women, and children. Accessories, underwear, yard supplies, draperies—everything and anything. Customers who shopped in the basement weren't second-class citizens, either. They could eat lunch there and even get their shoes shined. Dayton's also boasted what was described as a "generous" return policy.

The prospect of entertaining the customers brought all kinds of innovative ideas. For example, "Russian tea in true Russian style" was held on the third floor during fashion week, and Dayton's offered a five-week course in dressmaking, which three hundred Minneapolis women participated in, and which climaxed with a style show. But the "Little Mothers and Dolls Tea d'enfant" might have been the bravest. Three thousand girls ages three to twelve—without their mothers—were entertained during a two-hour event in which they drank "tiny cups of chocolate" and ate animal crackers without making so much as a peep.

Dayton's held its first "Jubilee Bargain Sale" on October 12, 1922, an occasion that saw the store sell double of what it had on the largest days it had previously experienced. The following day, the store placed an ad in the *Minneapolis Morning Tribune* thanking its customers and adding: "We appreciate the confidence of the people of Minneapolis in our advertising and our merchandise—it imposes on us a greater responsibility for the future. We will strive always to merit that confidence."

## Company Culture and Charity

Dayton ran the store like a family business, and his beliefs spilled over into his business principles, which followed a strict Presbyterian ethos: Dayton's wasn't open for business on Sundays, the store did not sell alcohol, it did not allow business travel or advertise on the Sabbath, and it would not advertise in a newspaper with liquor ads.

All the while, Dayton supported the community with his generosity and civic-minded efforts, which infused into the company's culture. By 1920, his store employed well over one thousand locals and held company-wide picnics on Lake Minnetonka in nearby Spring Park for over 1,700 Dayton employees and their guests. At Christmas, Dayton's awarded annual bonuses equivalent to 2 percent of the sales.

Later in Dayton's life, he spoke at Macalester College, a Presbyterian school in St. Paul, and delivered the following message, which offers insight into his philanthropic mind: "It sounds somewhat complex but really it is very simple. Business integrity can be defined to be: Doing things as you agreed to do them. Doing things when you agreed to do them. Doing the things that you ought to do."

Dayton's religious upbringing instilled habits such as regular church attendance, tithing, and reading the Bible. Even before wealth found him, Dayton regularly tithed. Later in his life, he would remind church ministers about their responsibility to exalt the virtues of tithing from the pulpit. By the time George had reached the age of thirty, he gave 40 percent of his income to his church. But his charity didn't stop there. Dayton regularly matched donations to charities as a means of incentivizing others to give.

In 1918, he established the Dayton Foundation, which he created with the basic aim of helping anybody in need. Though he directed much of his giving—both personally and through the foundation—toward religious matters, such as ministers, missionaries, and Macalester College, he also supported nonreligious entities in need.

Dayton saw fit to make sure the company donated to charitable causes too.

Because the company had not gone public, this was not an issue. The Minneapolis community viewed Dayton as a giver—someone who freely offered his money and time where matters of charity, public welfare, and religion were concerned. In addition to the Presbyterian Church, he was involved in the Minneapolis YWCA and the YMCA, the Union City Mission, and he also served as president of the board of trustees of Macalester, where he played a large role in the institution's development. Yet he considered using a majority of his personal fortune to establish the Dayton Foundation to be the most important achievement of his life.

After George Dayton's death on February 18, 1938, the Minneapolis Morning Tribune wrote the following morning: "In the more than 50 years that Minnesota knew him as a citizen, it had countless occasions manifested itself, not in idle words or ostentation, but in good deeds humbly done."

# The future is within reach.

When you start making your goals a top priority, everything falls into place. Learn from the leaders inspiring millions & apply their strategies to your professional journey.

Leadership Essentials Blog

Activate 180 Podcast

Interactive E-courses

Free templates

**LEADERSHIP ESSENTIALS**
by HarperCollins Leadership

For more business and leadership advice and resources, visit hcleadershipessentials.com.

9 781400 232758